Crown Hill Cemetery

The City on a Hill (Indianapolis, Indiana)

Joy Neighbors

America
Through
Time

America Through Time®
An imprint of Sutton Publishing Inc.
www.through-time.com

First published 2025

ISBN 978-1-63499-564-1

Typeset in 10pt on 13pt Sabon
Printed and bound in the United States of America

Contents

1
The History of Crown Hill Cemetery

Known as "The City on a Hill," Crown Hill Cemetery is located on the highest point of land in Indianapolis, Indiana. Today, more than 225,000 souls rest eternally in this serene 555-acre rural cemetery, known for its beauty and historical significance.

The stories and photos in this book provide an intimate look into the lives of past Indianapolis residents and the monuments, mausoleums, and markers that commemorate their final resting places.

In 1821, the new capital city was laid out within a square-mile radius in the middle of Indiana by Alexander Ralston, who also assisted in laying out the city's first cemetery, Greenlawn.

It was decided to establish a new cemetery outside of Indianapolis. On the selected site, strawberries grew in profusion, hence the name "Strawberry Hill." But a more dignified moniker was needed, something that matched the beauty of the land and foretold the dignity of its purpose. Based on the prominent 842-foot summit located on the property, the name chosen was Crown Hill. When the Articles of Association were signed on September 25, 1863, Crown Hill Cemetery, composed of 258-acres, was established as a private, nonprofit, nondenominational burial ground. On June 1, 1864, the cemetery was dedicated, and the first burial occurred the next day for thirty-three-year-old Lucy Ann Hart Seaton, who died of tuberculosis.

Fredrick Chislett was hired as the cemetery's first superintendent. He designed a modern "rural cemetery" that followed the contours of the rolling land creating a landscape where monuments and memorials blended seamlessly into the garden-like settings.

During the Civil War, Camp Morton, near Indianapolis, was designated as the main prisoner-of-war internment for Confederate soldiers. Due to the number of soldiers dying in the Civil War, federal officials requested that an acre-and-a-half be set aside as a national cemetery. This became the first of three military cemeteries located in Crown Hill and one of only two national military cemeteries in Indiana in 1866.

In 1875, a large two-story holding vault was constructed from Indiana limestone, with a chapel and ninety-six holding rooms. Designed in the Gothic Revival style by architect Diedrich Bohlen, the Gothic Chapel is now used for funerals, lectures, concerts, and weddings. The "back" entrance to the cemetery became the main entrance in 1885 when the Gothic Gate was installed.

Crown Hill Cemetery was designated a National Historic Place in 1973, and eleven years later, the Crown Hill Heritage Foundation was incorporated to preserve the cemetery's history and heritage. In 1988, the cemetery was honored as a "museum of state and local history." Today, Crown Hill is one of the largest non-governmental cemeteries in the country.

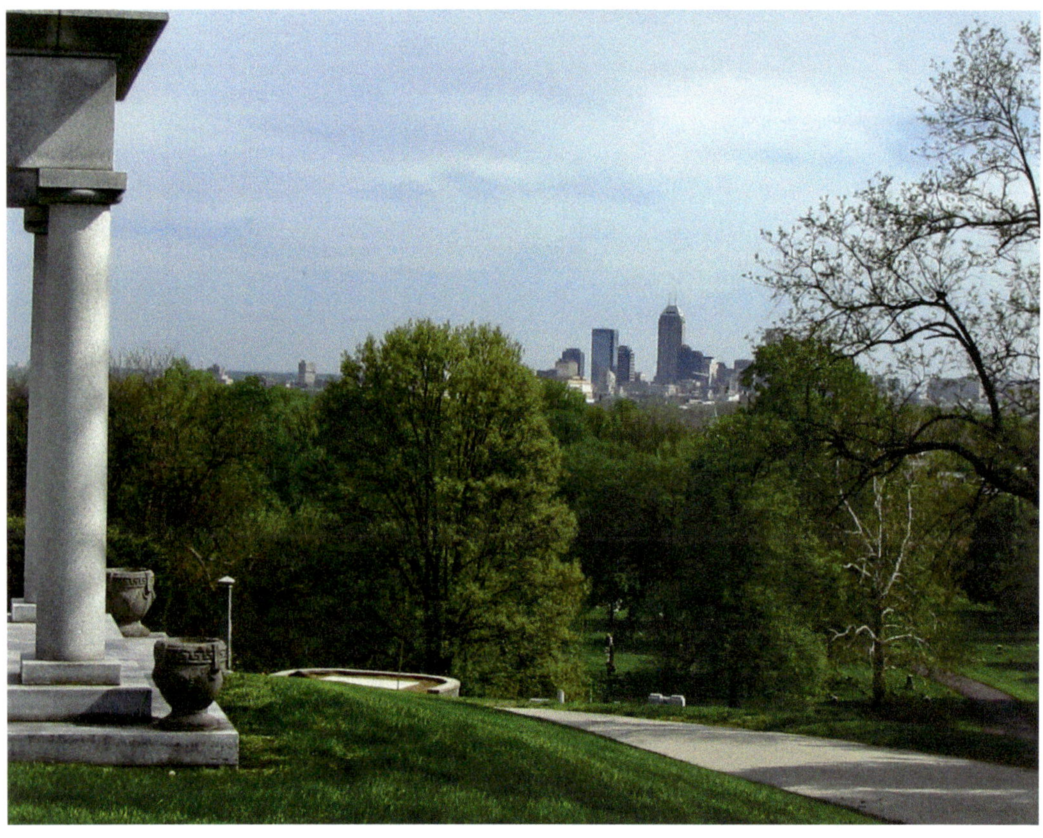

The skyline of Indianapolis, as seen from the James Whitcomb Riley monument "On the Crown," depicts a thriving city beyond the serenity of the cemetery. The lush green of spring shows that everywhere there is rebirth, even in Crown Hill.

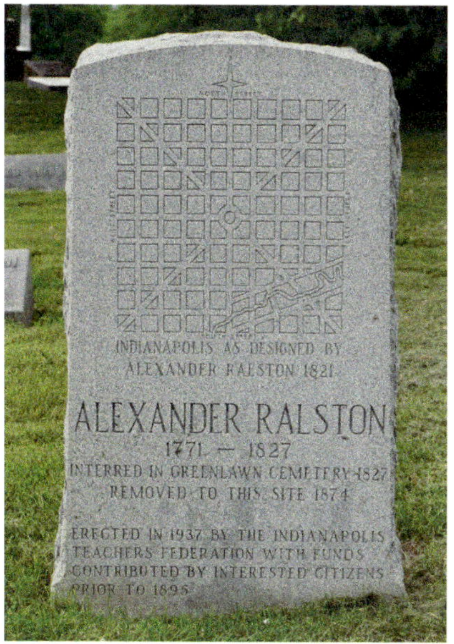

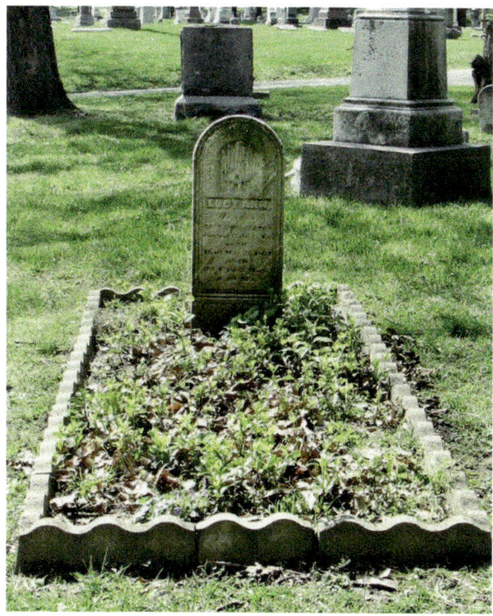

Above left: In 1821, surveyor Alexander Ralston (1771 – January 5, 1827) platted the capital city within a mile-square. His plat map of the city was etched onto his tombstone by the Indianapolis Teachers Federation in 1937. (Section 3, Lot 30)

Above right: Lucy Ann Hart Seaton (1831 – May 6, 1864), the first burial at Crown Hill Cemetery, has a simple marble stone with a "weeping willow tree," which symbolizes grief and rebirth, marking her grave. Her epitaph reads, "Lucy, God grant I may meet you in heaven." Four months later, Seaton's daughter, also named Lucy, died and was buried alongside her mother. (Section 4, Lot 28)

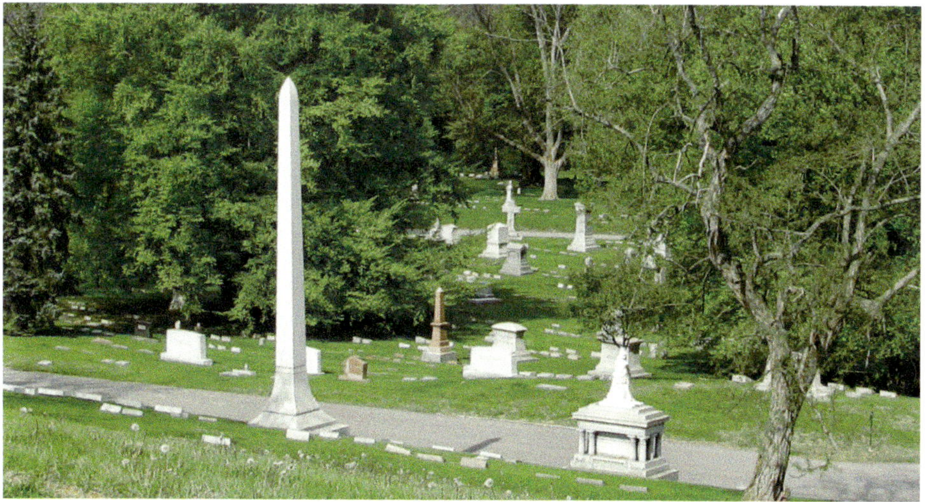

Standing "On the Crown" provides a beautiful view of stones, markers, and monuments in a cemetery that was designed in the "rural cemetery style."

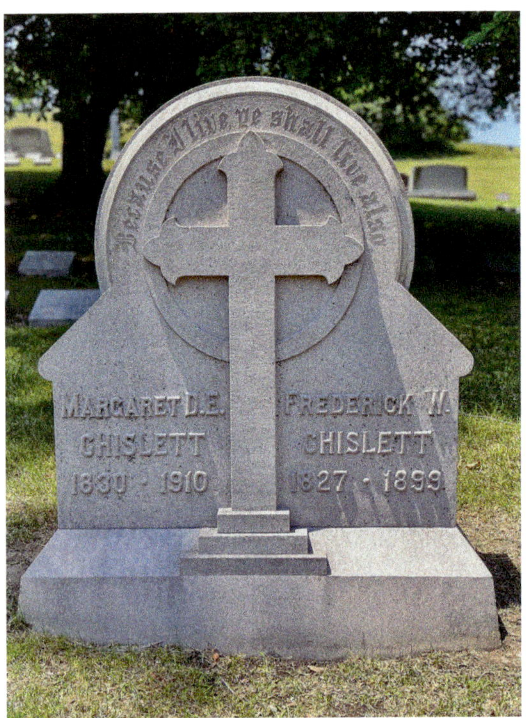

Left: Fredrick Chislett (1827 – November 9, 1899), the first cemetery superintendent, has a Latin cross for his marker with *fleur de lis* ends. The cross stands on three bases representing the Holy Trinity. (Section 14, Lot 14)

Below: Crown Hill National Cemetery is the resting place of more than 2,000 military personnel, most from the Civil War. Individual flags are placed beside each white government-issued marble stone every Memorial Day. The first Decoration (Memorial) Day service was held on May 30, 1868, and it continues, making it the longest consecutively held Memorial Day remembrance event in Indiana. (Sections 9 & 10)

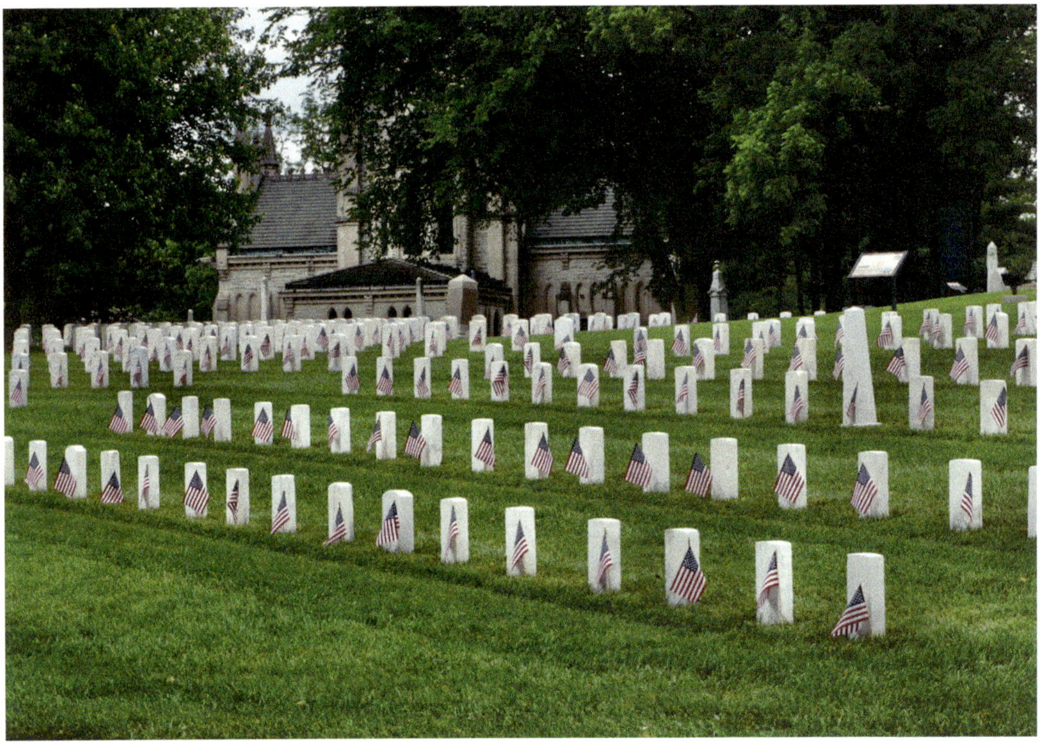

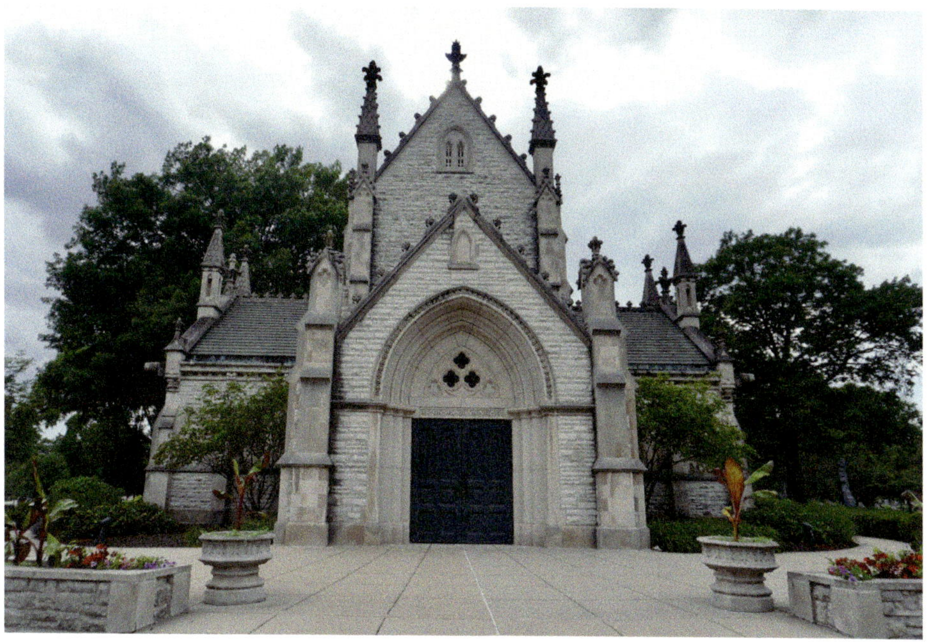

The Gothic Chapel was initially called the Gothic Vault. Designed in the Gothic Revival style by architect Diedrich Bohlen in 1875, it is used today for events and concerts. (Section 9)

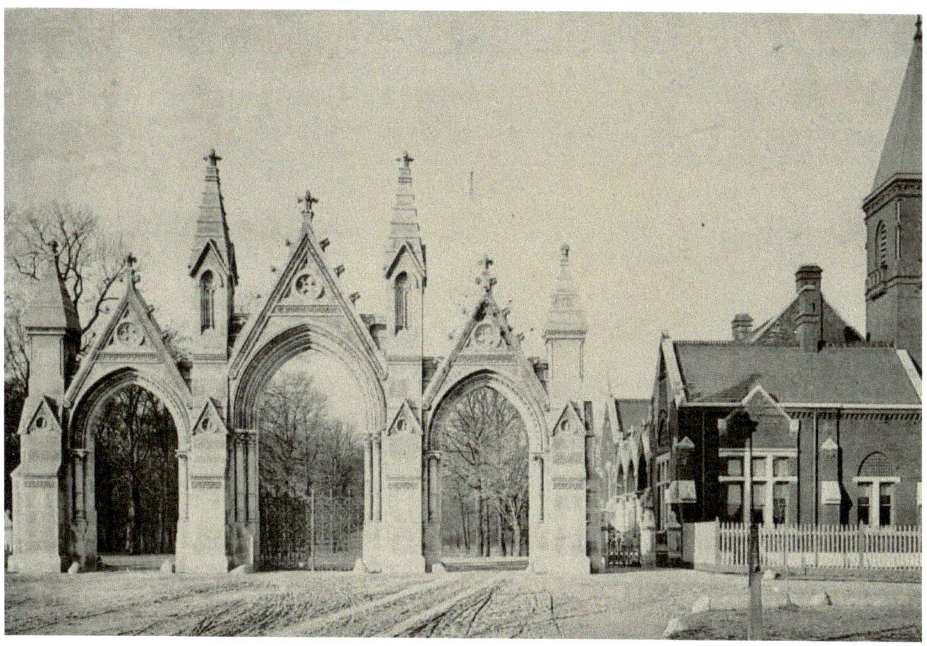

Built in 1885, the Gothic Gates became the main entrance to the cemetery. The Waiting Station was where visitors would wait for friends to attend a funeral or after the service. An upstairs apartment provided a home for the caretaker. *[Indiana Historical Society]*

2

Crown Hill Founding Fathers

Several prominent Indianapolis businessmen played a part in the founding of Crown Hill. Among those who provided key contributions were James Blake, Calvin Fletcher, and James Ray.

Each man had a huge part in the development of Indianapolis as a city. Blake built the first steam mill, established the first dry goods store, and was involved in establishing "Greenlawn," the city's first cemetery, in 1821. Later, he determined that a new, spacious burial ground was necessary to meet the needs of the growing city. Blake served on the Crown Hill Board until his death.

Calvin Fletcher assisted in funding the acquisition of Crown Hill, and James Ray was appointed president of the Crown Hill Association Board of Corporators in 1863, a position he held until his death.

Ovid Butler and Dr. John Kitchen also played active roles in the cemetery's establishment. Butler was one of the original incorporators of Crown Hill and served on the board until his death. Kitchen was also an original board member and took an active part in fencing the grounds. He was also involved in governing the cemetery.

Thanks to these farsighted individuals, Crown Hill remains one of the largest and most historic cemeteries in the country. With more than 555-acres of picturesque grounds, structures, and roadways, the cemetery continues to provide a serene and distinguished place for all to be buried.

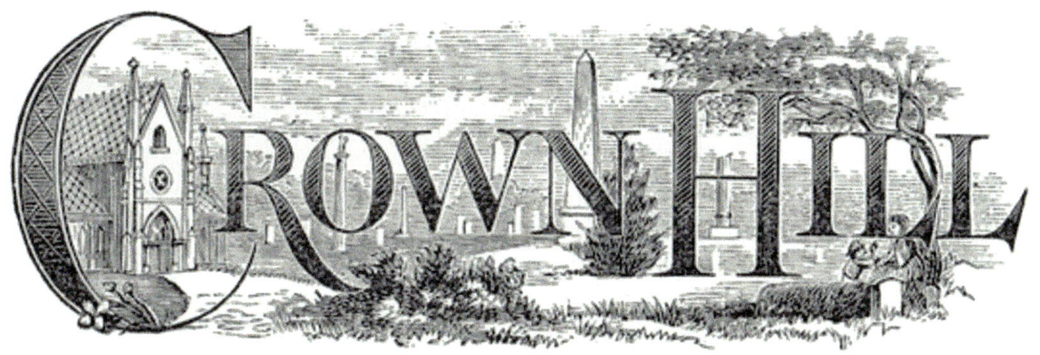

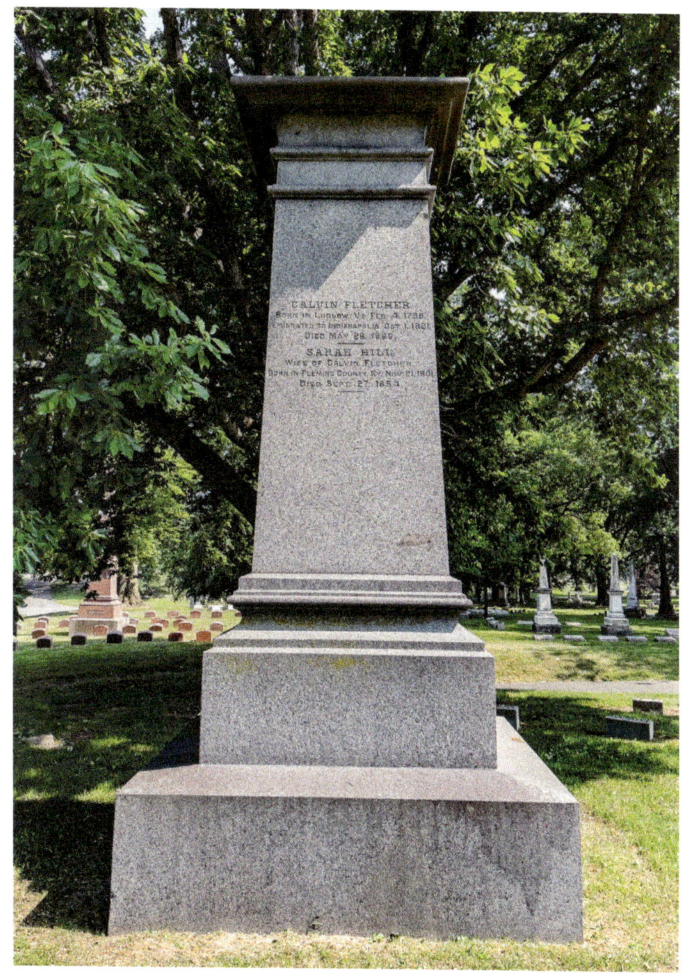

Above: The Crown Hill Cemetery logo from 1875. [*Crown Hill Heritage Foundation*]

Right: Calvin Fletcher (February 4, 1798 – May 26, 1866) served as an Indiana State Senator and helped advance U.S. Colored Troops during the Civil War in Indiana. Fletcher was a driving force in funding the purchase of the Crown Hill property. (Section7, Lot 4) *[Crown Hill Heritage Society]*

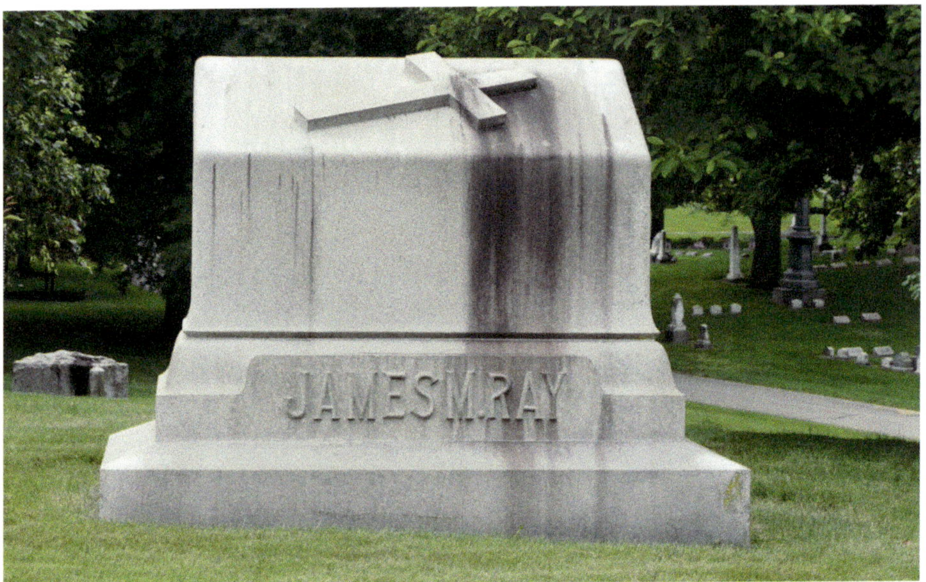

James M. Ray (November 25, 1808 – February 22, 1881) spear-headed the founding of Crown Hill. He also served with the Indianapolis Benevolent Society, the State Blind School, and the Indianapolis Female Institute. His grave is marked with a Latin cross placed at an angle on top of his stone. (Section 1, Lot 70)

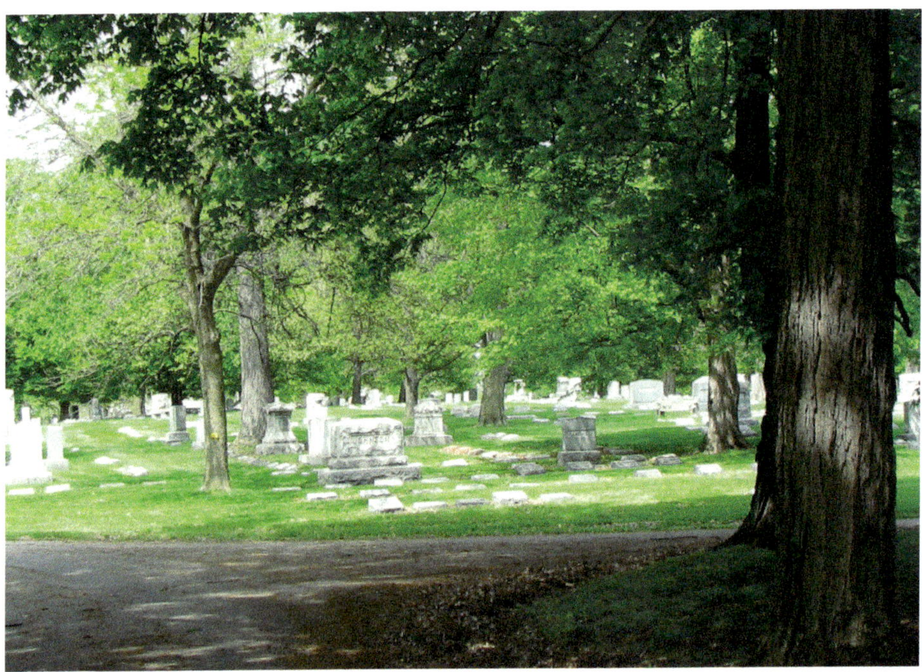

The Rural Cemetery grounds provided a pleasant place to stroll and escape the dirt and fumes of the city.

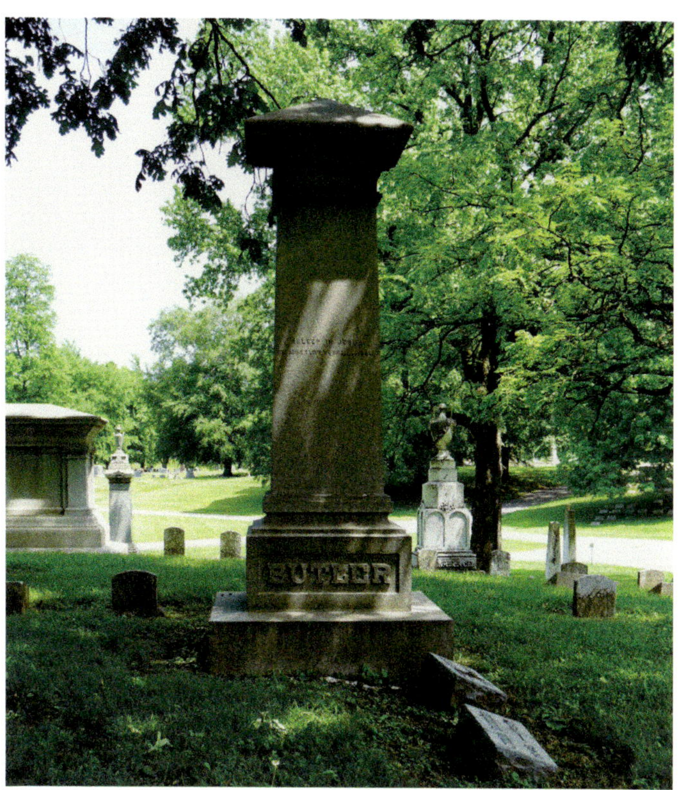

Right: Ovid Butler (February 7, 1801 – July 12, 1881) founded North Western Christian College, the second university in the state. His tall monument is inscribed, "Asleep in Jesus. Because I live ye shall live also." (Section 6, Lot 14)

Below: Dr. John M. Kitchen (July 12, 1826 – February 6, 1916) played a key role in the development of the cemetery. His crypt, built of marble blocks, was the second mausoleum to be built on the grounds, but the only one to be constructed on the side of a hill. It was sealed in 1959. (Section 6, Mausoleum)

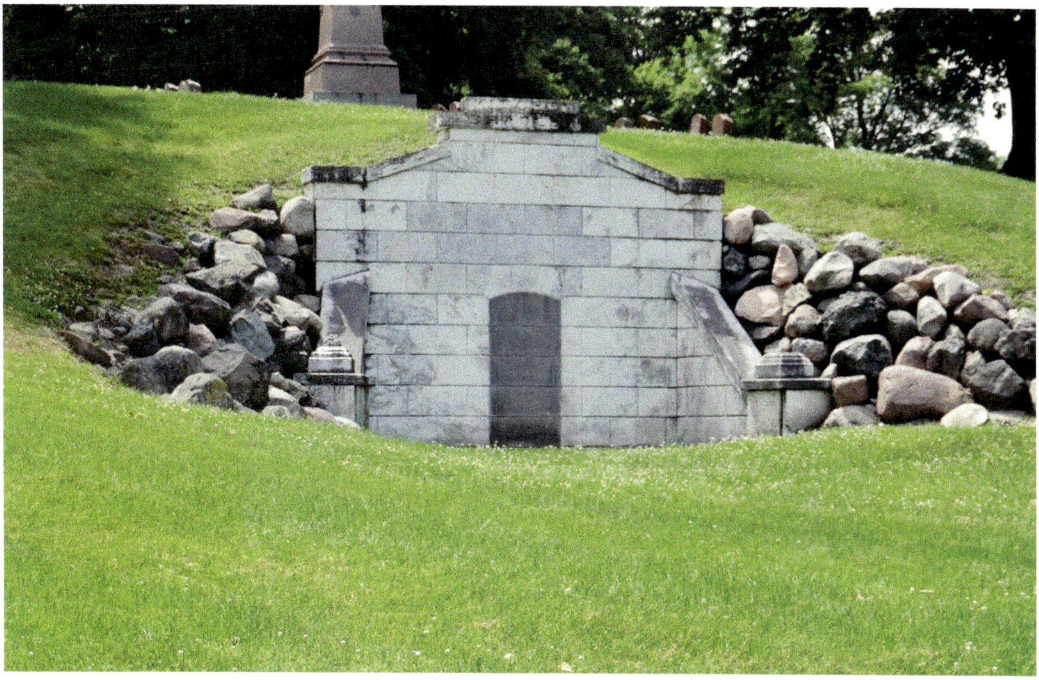

3

Indianapolis Pioneers

Indianapolis became a haven for pioneer families looking for flat, fertile ground to farm. The White River supplied the power to run early grist and flour mills, which provided jobs for the growing population and kept the community fed. The town grew quickly, and by 1824, it was selected to be the seat of state government, taking that honor away from the southern Indiana town of Corydon. On January 1, 1825, Indianapolis became the capital of Indiana, thanks in part to Samuel Merrill, a successful politician who worked tirelessly to get the state capital moved north to Indianapolis.

Nicholas McCarty, along with cemetery founders Blake and Ray, started the Indianapolis Steam Flour Mill Company, which advanced local industry. Nathaniel Bolton was the editor of Indianapolis' first newspaper, the *Indianapolis Gazette.* He served as Indiana State Librarian from 1851 until 1855, when he was appointed consul to Geneva, Switzerland, by President Franklin Pierce. Dr. Isaac Coe was the first doctor in Indianapolis to have a medical license. In 1821, he brought the city through a malaria epidemic with only seventy-two deaths, one-eighth of the population.

Crown Hill has rescued two pioneer graveyards from vanishing, due to neglect and industry expansion. These Hoosier settlers have been reinterred in the Pioneer Cemetery, located in the northern corner of Crown Hill. Monuments that identify the reinterred came from Rhoads Cemetery and Wright-Whitesell-Gentry Cemetery. Another 1,160 pioneers were moved here from Greenlawn Cemetery, the city's first burial ground.

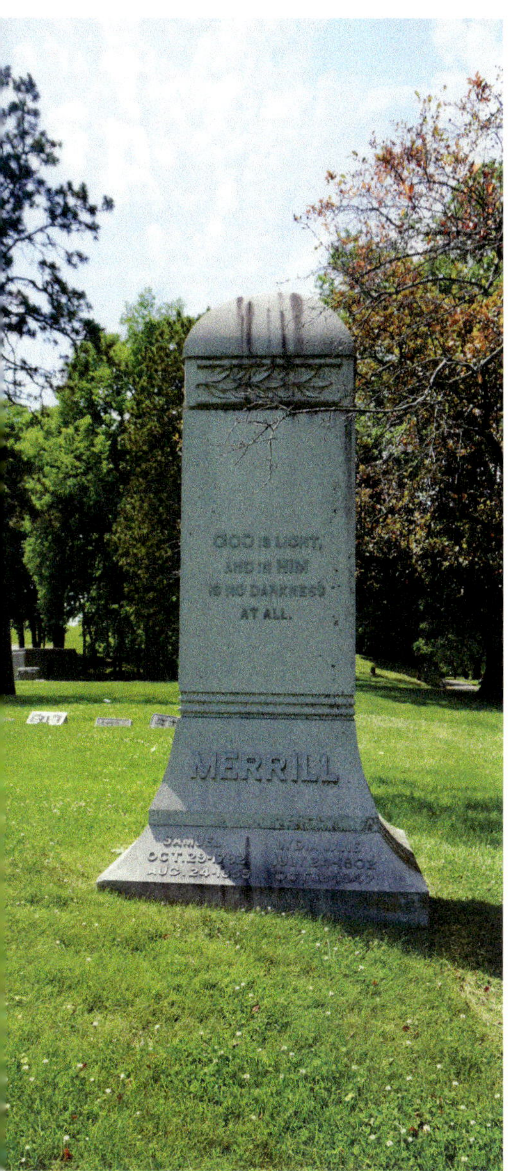

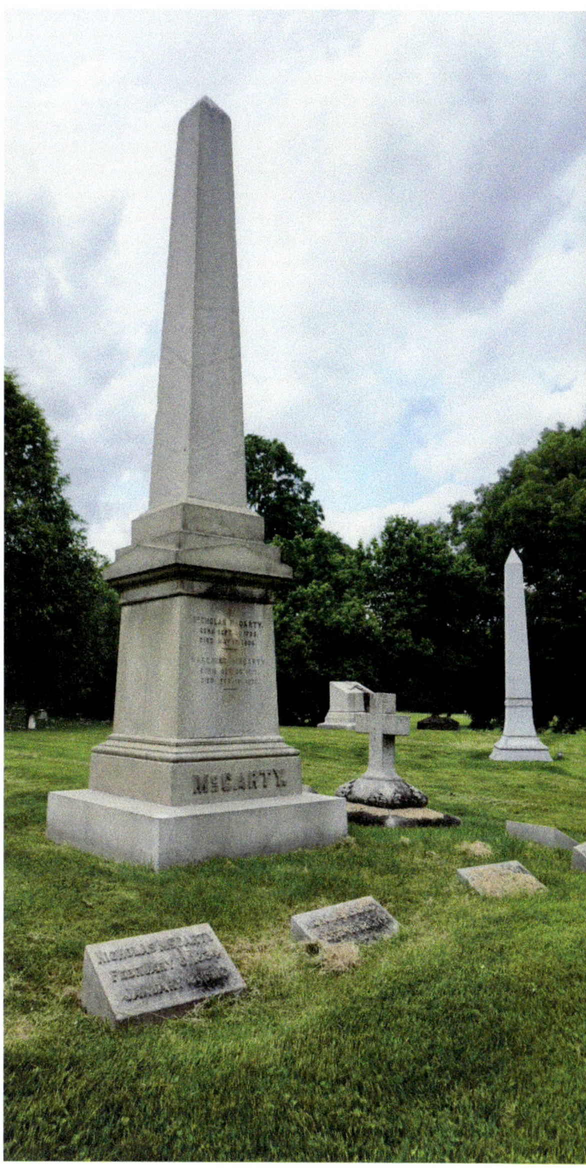

Above left: Samuel Merrill (October 29, 1792 – August 24, 1855) was instrumental in moving the state capital from Corydon to the new city of Indianapolis. Merrill then served as the Indiana State Treasurer. The Merrill monument is granite and features the epitaph, "God is light, and in him is no darkness at all." (Section 7, Lot 16)

Above right: Nicholas McCarty (September 26, 1795 – May 17, 1845) was one of Crown Hill Cemetery's administrators. McCarty served as a state senator and city councilman before founding the Indianapolis Orphans Home. His square-tapered obelisk bears the names and dates for him and his wife. (Section 1, Lot 71)

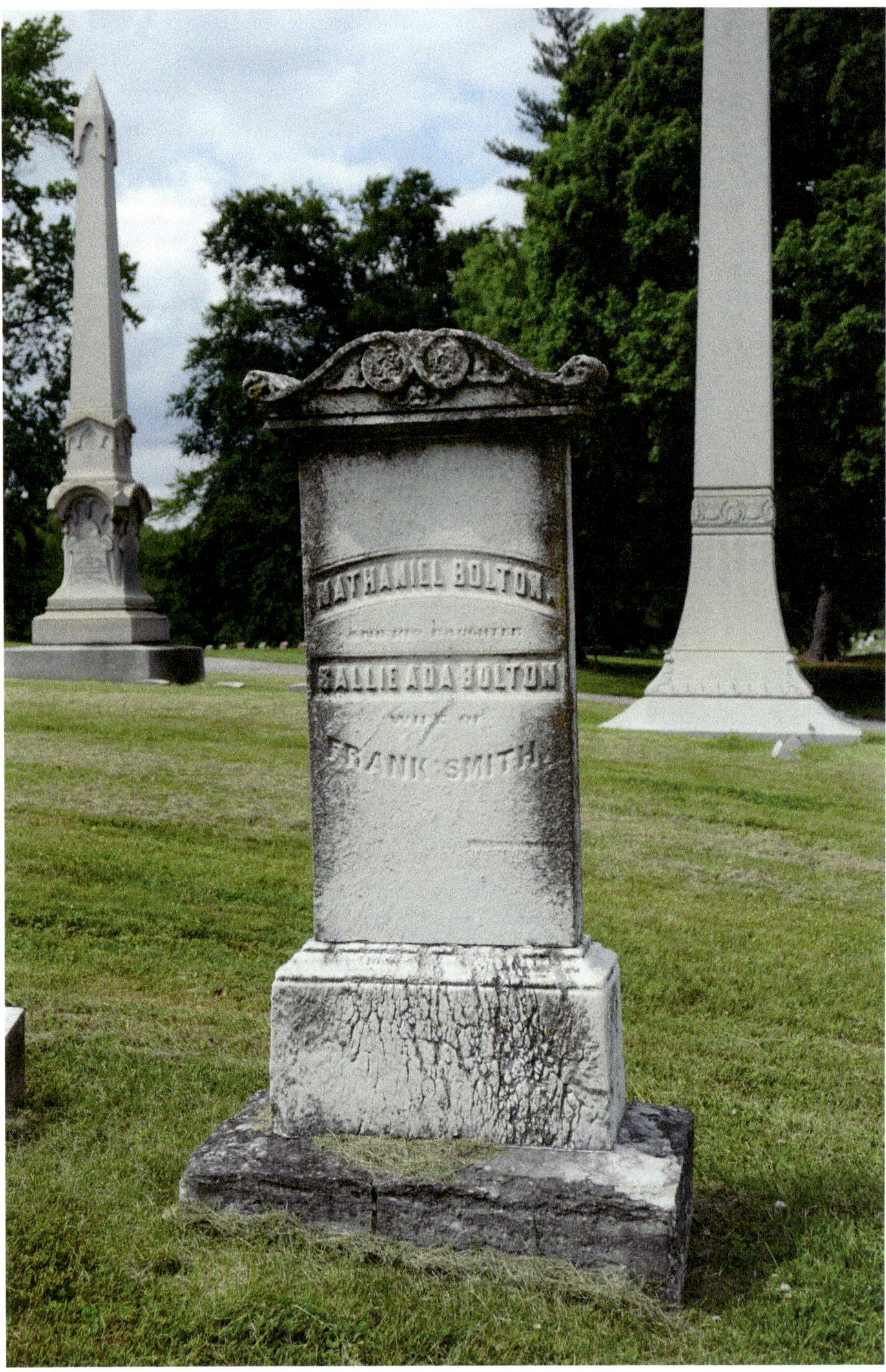

Nathaniel Bolton (July 25, 1803 – November 26, 1858) was editor of Indianapolis' first newspaper and served as the state librarian in 1851. Bolton's tall stone is of a simple design, harkening back to an eighteenth-century style. (Section 5, Lot 14)

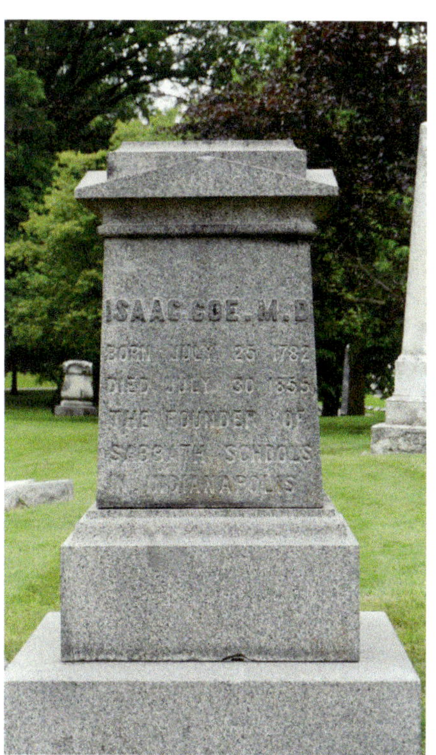

Right: Dr. Isaac Coe (July 25, 1782 – July 30, 1855) was the first licensed doctor in Indianapolis. Dr. Coe founded the first Sabbath schools (Sunday schools) in Indianapolis. His grave marker pays tribute to that: "The Founder of Sabbath Schools in Indianapolis." (Section 1, Lot 67)

Below: The Pioneer Cemetery contains the remains of 2,000 early settlers from three graveyards: Greenlawn, Rhodes, and Wright-Whitesell-Gentry Cemetery. Of the 1,160 pioneers reinterred from the city's first graveyard, Greenlawn Cemetery, only thirty-five were identified by name.

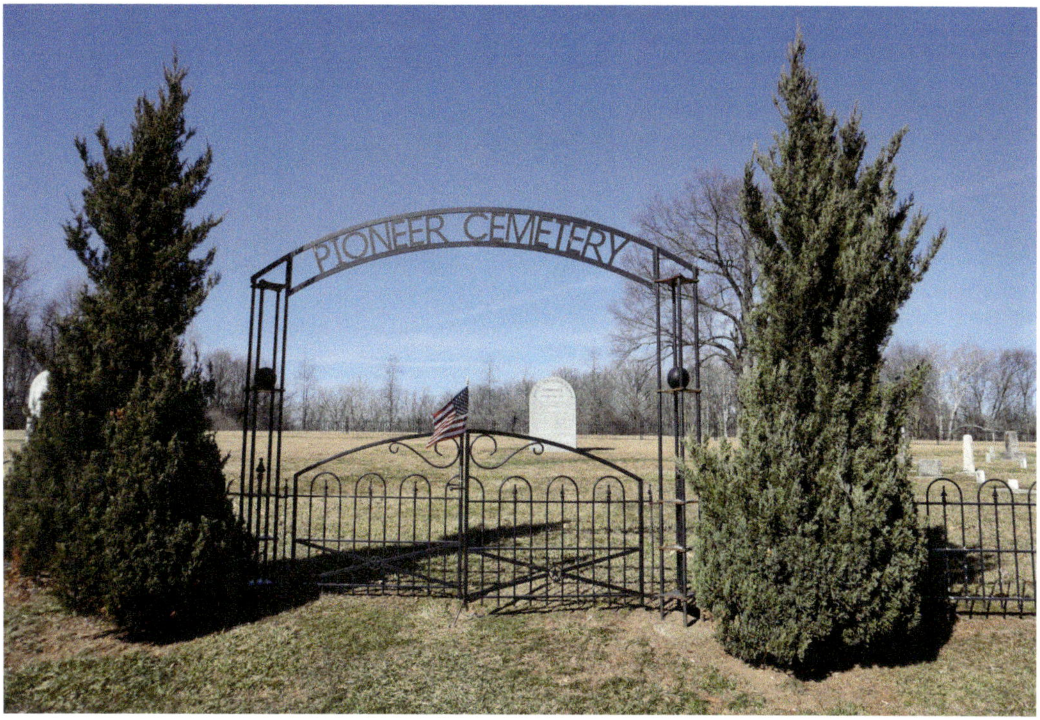

4
Those Who Served

Crown Hill is home to three national cemeteries with twenty-three acres dedicated to veterans. More than 700 Civil War soldiers, originally buried in the deteriorating Greenlawn Cemetery, were moved to Crown Hill National Cemetery after the war.

Confederate Mound is the second national cemetery in Crown Hill. It is the final resting place of 1,616 Confederate prisoners of war, most of whom died at Camp Morton. These soldiers were originally interred in Greenlawn Cemetery but were transferred to Crown Hill in 1931.

The Field of Valor Memorial is the third national cemetery and is dedicated to veterans and active-duty military personnel. It features Eagle Plaza and an Eternal Flame, along with the flags of the Armed Services.

Revolutionary War Soldiers

Crown Hill has two Revolutionary War veterans. Sergeant John Morrow was wounded at the Battle of Long Island and later reinterred at Crown Hill National Cemetery. Private Hezekiah Smith served with the Massachusetts Militia. He was moved to Crown Hill from Trader's Point.

Civil War Soldiers

The National Cemetery spans nearly an acre-and-a-half of individually marked graves. Bronze plaques with verses from Theodore O'Hara's poem, "Bivouac of the Dead," surround the outer edges of the grounds.

Private Edward Black was the youngest to serve in the Civil War, and in the United States. At eight-years-old, he enlisted as a Union drummer boy and mustered out in 1866. Black died seven years later of injuries sustained during the war. His drum is preserved at the Indianapolis Children's Museum.

Crown Hill is the resting place of seventeen Civil War generals, including one who bore the same name as the president of the Confederacy. Brigadier General Jefferson C. Davis is infamously known for killing his superior officer, General William "Bull" Nelson, and avoiding conviction due to Indiana Governor Oliver Morton's intervention. Davis remained in the military until his death.

Brigadier General Robert Foster served in the Civil War. Afterwards, he served on the commission that tried and found President Abraham Lincoln's assassination conspirators guilty. Foster was Indiana's first junior vice commander-in-chief for the Indiana Grand Army of the Republic (GAR) at the nation's first encampment in 1866.

In 1862, Dr. Richard J. Gatling invented the Gatling gun, a six-barreled, hand-cranked machine gun that could fire up to 200 rounds per minute. By 1882, it fired 1,200 rounds per minute, and was a major advancement in weaponry. The U.S. Army used the Gatling gun during the Spanish-American War, but it was considered obsolete by 1911.

U.S. Colored Troops

Two-hundred-seventeen African Americans were buried in the U.S. Colored Troops section of the Crown Hill National Cemetery, including Sergeant Charles Brown, who served with Company A of the U.S. Colored Troops during the Civil War. After the war, he organized an African American branch of the GAR (Grand Army of the Republic). He was elected Junior Vice Department Commander, the highest post held by an African American, in 1901. Brown was a member of the "Colored Marching Club."

Private Milton Robinson, once enslaved, escaped the South with assistance from Indiana troops. Robinson enlisted in the Union Army and served with the 54th Massachusetts Volunteer Infantry. He was also a member of the African American Grand Army of the Republic (GAR).

Other Wars

Major General Edward R. S. Canby was the only general killed in the post-Civil War American Indian Wars when he was shot between the eyes by Captain Jack, chief of the Modoc Indians, during peace talks. Second Lieutenant Ralph Miller served nearly four years in the Philippines before being killed at the Presidio of San Francisco. He was given a military burial.

Major Harold Megrew served with the 161st Indiana Volunteer Infantry during the Spanish-American War. Megrew died in 1908, and his eye-catching monument was erected by United Spanish War Veterans in honor of his service as the first Commander-in-Chief of the U.S. Spanish War Veterans. The square bronze cross represents the four branches of service, crossed swords for cavalry, crossed rifles for infantry, crossed cannons for artillery, and an anchor for marines and sailors. Depicted inside the cross are soldiers bearing arms.

World War One aviation pioneer John H. Geisse worked as chief engineer of the Navy Aeronautical Engine Laboratory. His contributions to aviation included organizing airport construction, designing the tri-cycle undercarriage, and creating a flight simulator that accounted for kinesthetic cues during flight. He also invented the Geisse Cross-Wing Landing Gear and crafted the first electrical wing de-icing system.

Colonel James Kasler, a combat veteran of World War II, the Korean War, and the Vietnam War, was a highly decorated officer in the United States Air Force. He remains the only person ever awarded the Air Force Cross for bravery and heroism during extreme combat and as a prisoner-of-war in Vietnam. Kasler also received eleven Air Medals, nine Distinguished Flying Crosses, two Purple Hearts, two Silver Stars, two Bronze Stars, and a Legion of Merit.

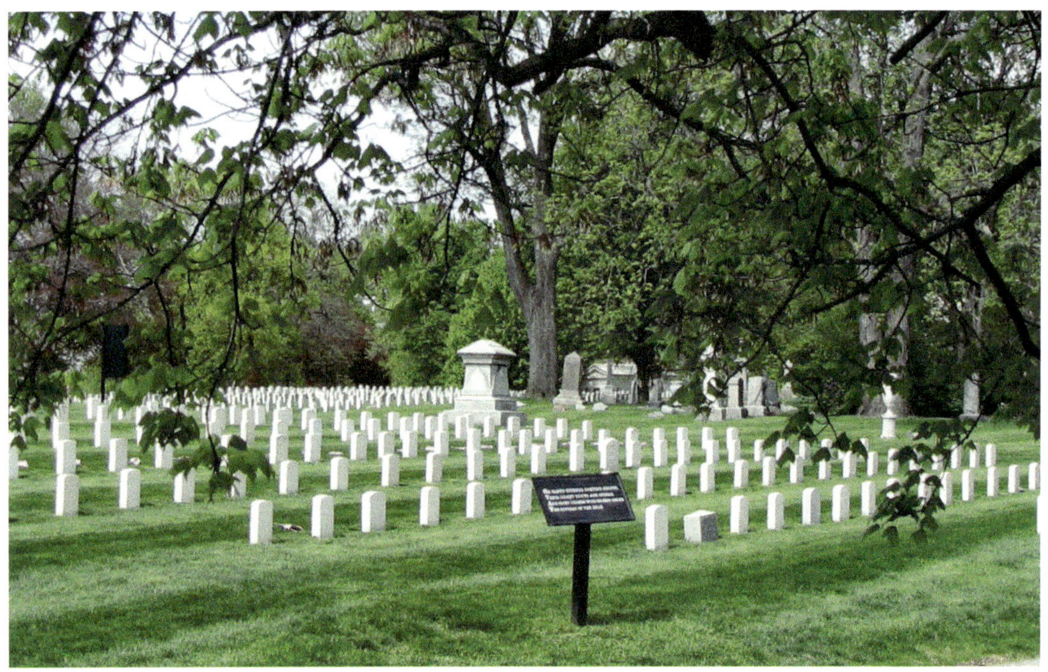

Nearly seventy-five percent of those buried in Crown Hill National Cemetery fought in the Civil War. Bronze plaques with verses from Theodore O'Hara's poem, "Bivouac of the Dead," surround the outer edges of the grounds. Today, the cemetery is home to three national cemeteries. (Sections 9 & 10)

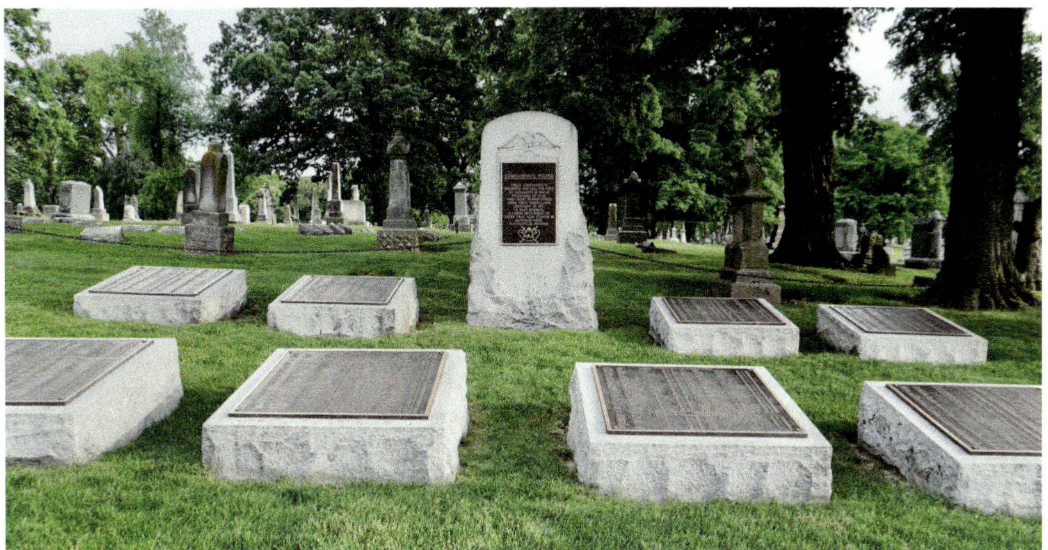

Confederate Mound is the final resting place of 1,616 Confederate soldiers. A central monument contains a plaque dedicated to the Confederate soldiers who died near Indianapolis during the Civil War. The ten bronze plaques mounted on granite stones list the names of Confederate soldiers who died at prisoner-of-war Camp Morton during the war. (Section 32, Lot 285)

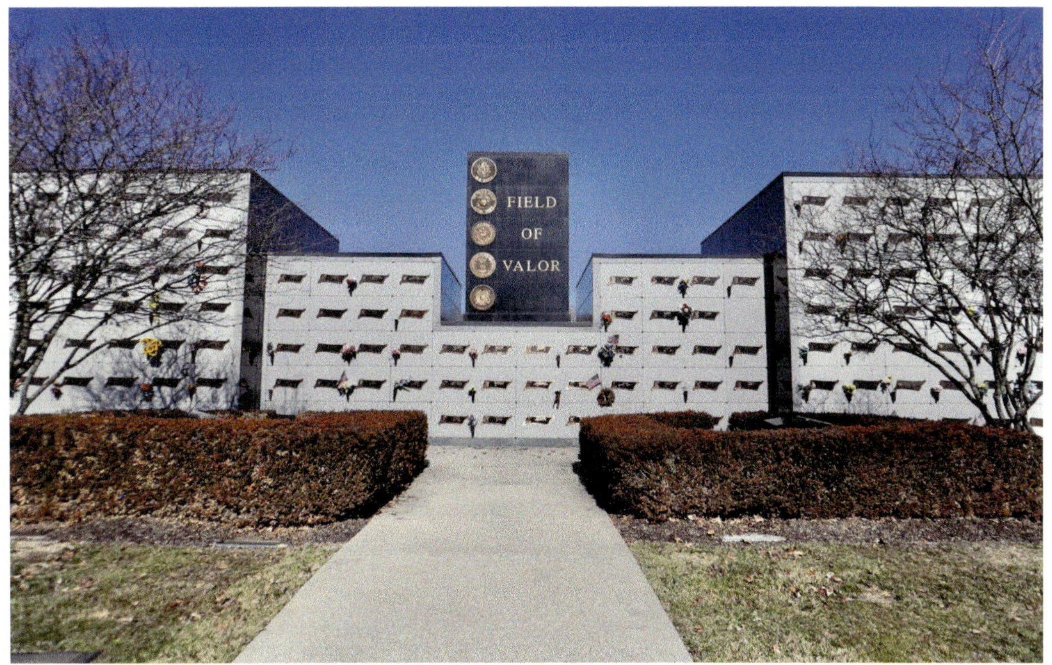

The Field of Valor Memorial and Mausoleum includes Eagle Plaza and an Eternal Flame that burns in remembrance of those who served. Bronze plaques list the names and dates of each soldier interred in the outdoor mausoleum. (Section 28)

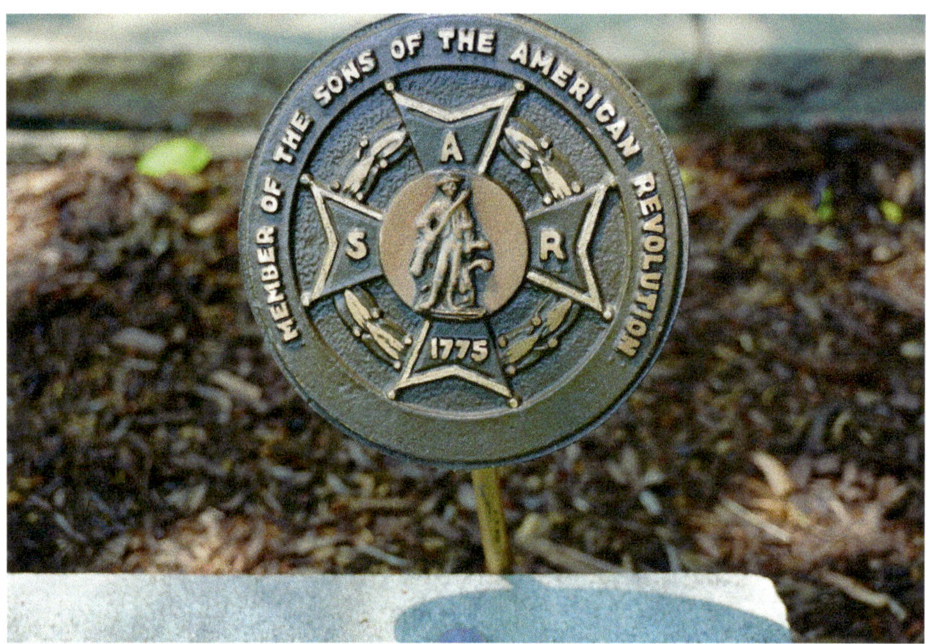

The Sons of the American Revolution (SAR) emblem features a four-armed cross with eight points. In the middle is the image of George Washington. The two American Revolutionary soldiers buried in Crown Hill are Orderly Sergeant John Morrow, buried in *Section 9, Lot 14*. Private Hezekiah Smith lies in Section 2, Lot 135.

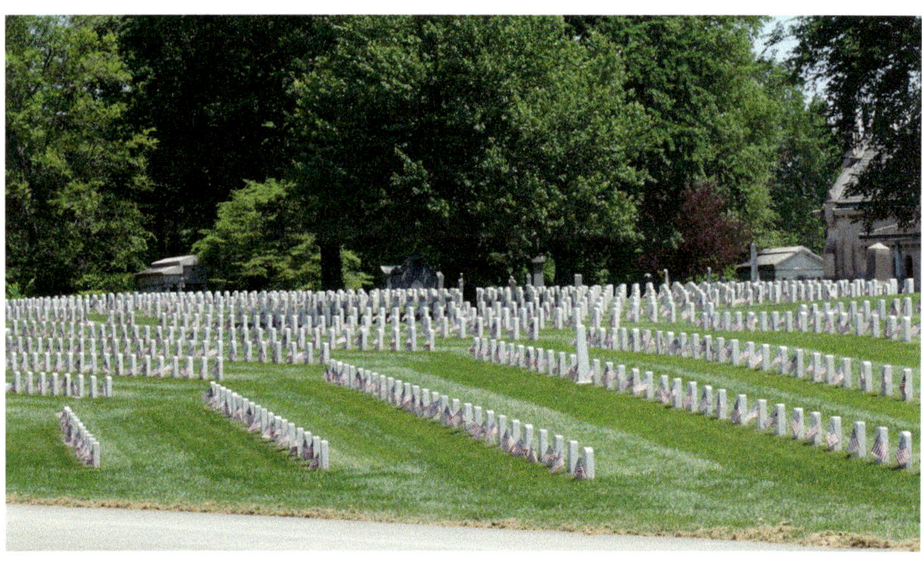

Crown Hill National Cemetery was established in 1866 on an acre-and-a-half of ground. The first 712 soldiers buried here were from Greenlawn Cemetery, along with 217 soldiers who were members of the United States Colored Troops. The last Union veteran burial took place in 1898. The National Cemetery is on the National Register of Historic Places.

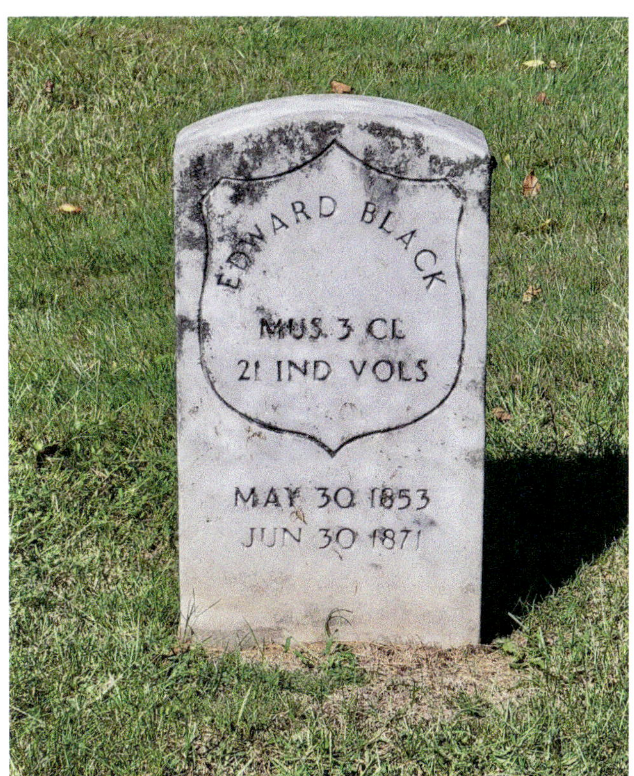

Eight-year-old Private Edward Black (May 30, 1853 – June 30, 1872) is believed to be the youngest soldier to serve the United States and the youngest to serve in the Civil War. A white marble military stone marks his grave in another part of the cemetery. (Section 16, Lot 148) *[Alessa Kivlehen]*

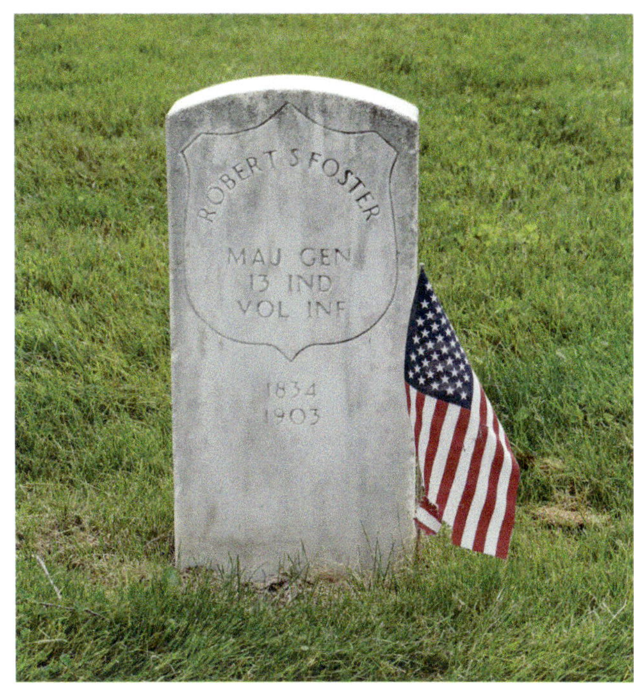

Brigadier General Robert Foster (January 27, 1834 – March 3, 1903) served in President Abraham Lincoln's administration. Foster's grave is marked with a military-issued white marble stone. (Section 15, Lot 1)

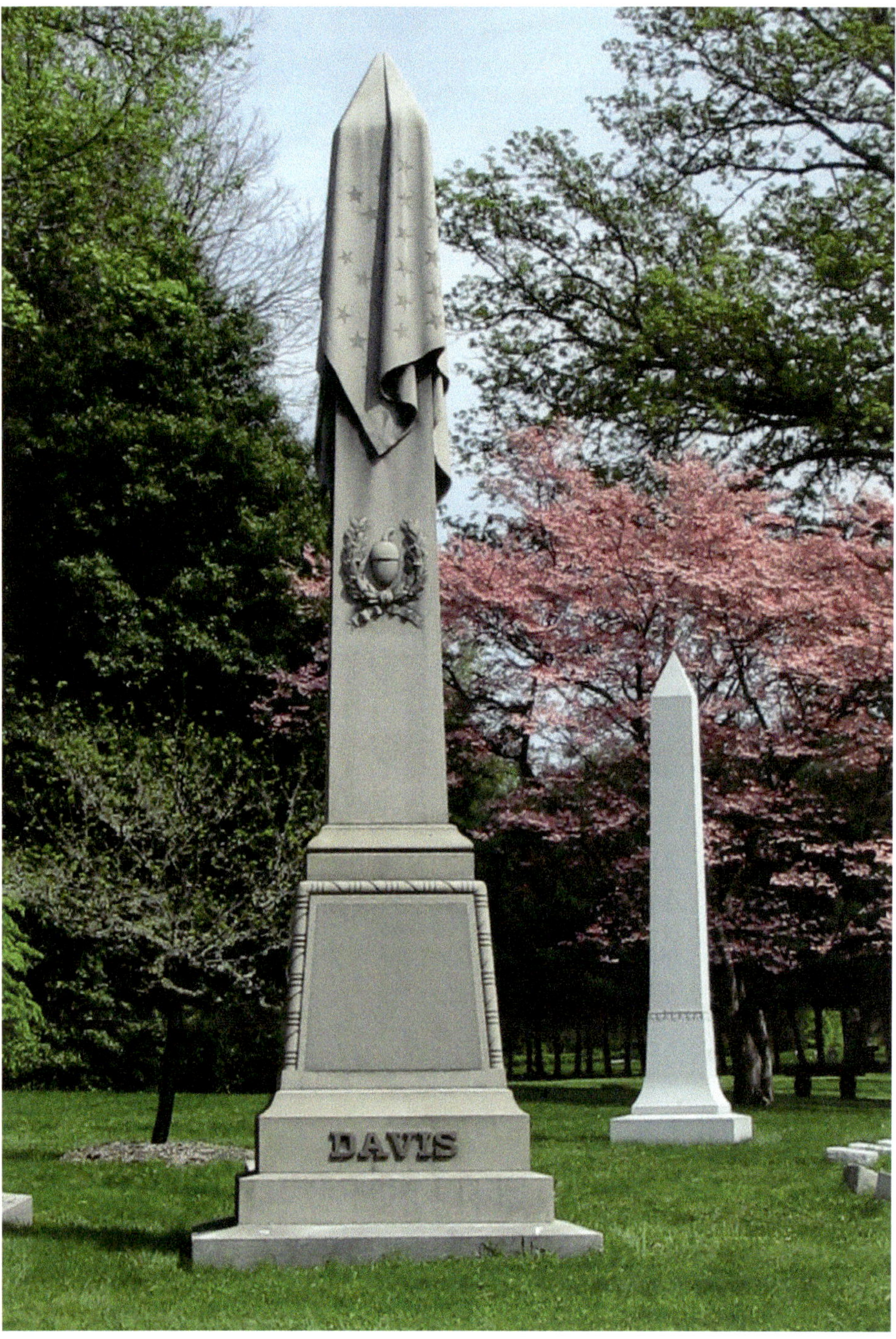

Brigadier General Jefferson C. Davis (March 2, 1828 – November 30, 1879) served as a Union commander but is remembered for killing a superior officer. His obelisk marker is draped in a granite American flag, and his stone is adorned with an acorn for prosperity and laurel for victory over death. (Section 29, Lot 1)

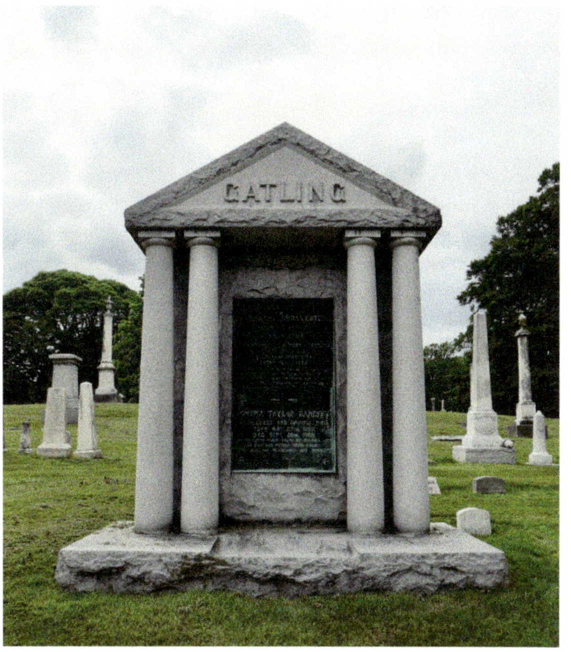

Right: Dr. Richard Gatling (September 12, 1818 – February 26, 1903) invented the Gatling gun. The front of his monument resembles a mausoleum, but in actuality, it is a tall granite stone with four Doric columns that set off a bronze plaque. (Section 3, Lot 9)

Below: Those who served in the United States Colored Troops (USCT) fought in numerous battles, including the Battle of Crater, the Battle of Chaffin's Farm, and the Battle of Appomattox Court House. Close to 200,000 men served with the USCT, about ten percent of the Union Army's total personnel. (Section 10)

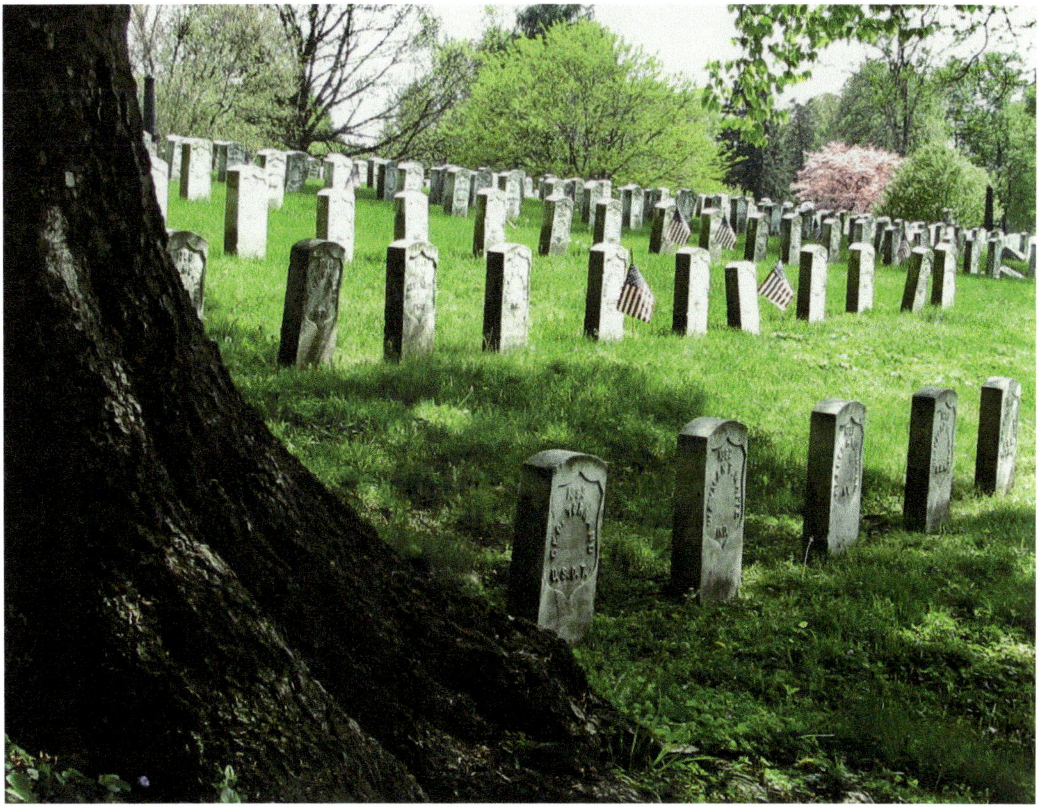

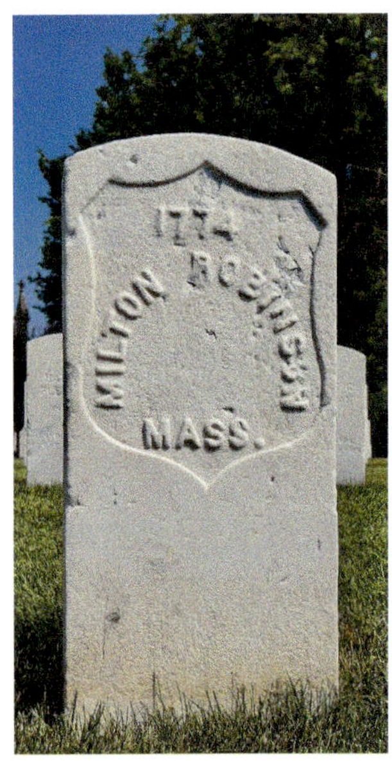

Left: Private Milton Robinson (1840 – 1930) was an escaped slave who served in the Union Army. Robinson was a member of the African American GAR (Grand Army of the Republic.) His stone is of military-issued white marble. (Section 9, Lot 177)

Below: Lieutenant Ralph Miller (February 3, 1874 – August 13, 1903) was killed at the Presidio of San Francisco. His monument is engraved with two crossed swords, which signify he died in battle. A granite American flag is draped over the stone for mourning. Engraved upon the stone are the details of his service and details of his death. (Section 21, Lot 1)

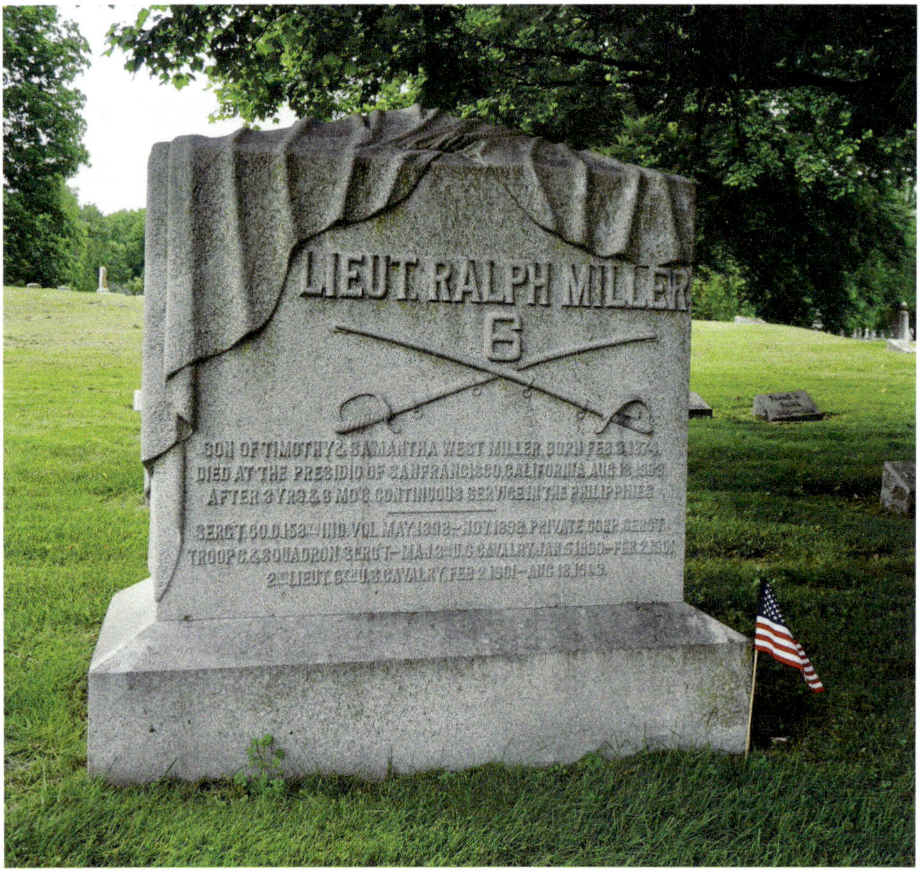

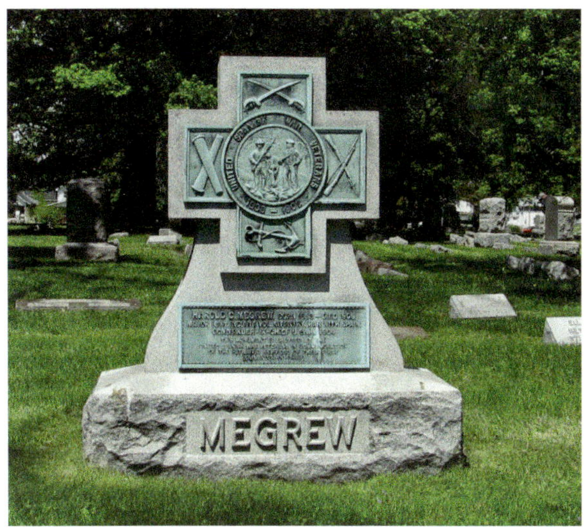

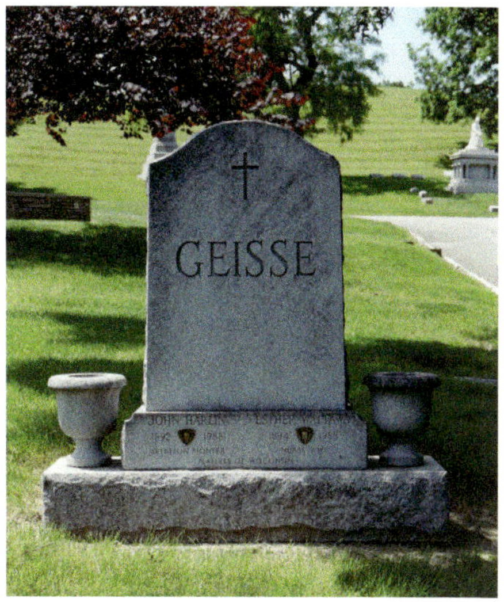

Above left: Major Harold Megrew (March 16, 1858 – April 26, 1908) served during the Spanish-American War. The United Spanish War Veterans erected this monument for Megrew to honor his patriotic service as their "first commander in chief." (Section 47, Lot 36)

Above right: Aviation pioneer Second Lieutenant John Harlan Geisse (July 17, 1892 – December 4, 1988) was a chief engineer at the Navy Aeronautical Engine Laboratory. He developed numerous aviation engineering systems and programs, and his stone denotes his status as an aviation pioneer. (Section 13, Lot 20)

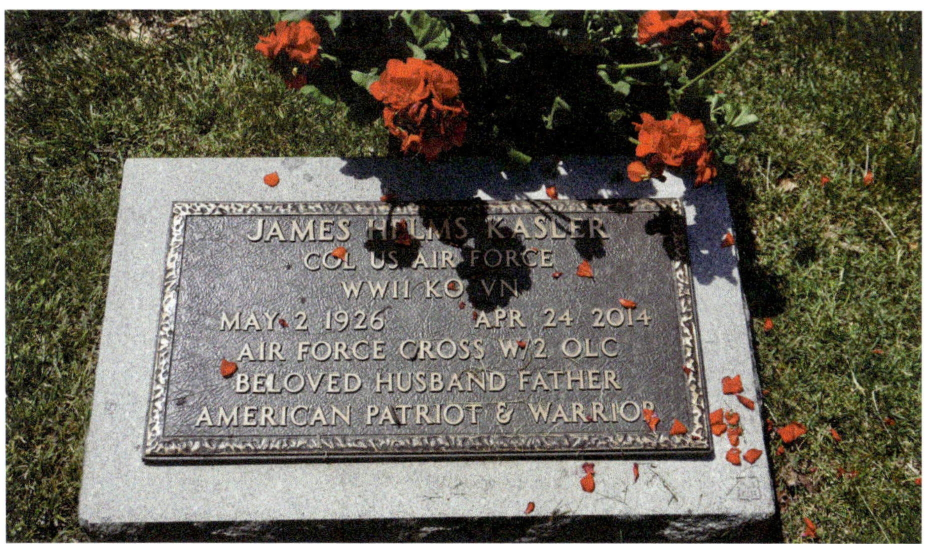

A combat veteran of three wars, Colonel James Kasler *(May 2, 1926 – April 24, 2014)* became the fifteenth jet "ace" in Korea and was awarded the Air Force Cross three times, an award which is second only to the Medal of Honor for extraordinary heroism in combat. He is remembered on his marker as an "American patriot and warrior." (Section 61, Lot 13)

5

Movers and Shakers

The Cambridge Dictionary defines a mover and shaker as "someone willing to make big changes to get things done." Indianapolis has had its share of "movers and shakers." Whether in the field of law, business, or education, a multitude of people have made significant impacts on this community, state, and nation.

In the legal field, Robert Brokenburr stood out. Brokenburr worked as deputy prosecutor for Marion County and was the first African American elected to the Indiana Senate. Another attorney, James Thomas Vastine (T.V.) Hill was also a trailblazer for African American rights. When Hill died in 1928, his "firsts" were etched on his stone, and he was remembered as " ... the Dean of Negro Lawyers."

Innovators and educators collaborated to develop and shape their city's reputation in the twentieth century. William G. Mays worked for several large companies, including Eli Lilly, Procter & Gamble, and Cummins Engine Company, before becoming president of Specialty Chemicals in 1977. In 1980, he founded Mays Chemical Company, which became one of the largest chemical distribution facilities in the country. In 1990, he delved into media and purchased the *Indianapolis Recorder*, one of the oldest African American newspapers in the U.S. Mays received the Madame C. J. Walker Lifetime Achievement Award and the United Negro College Fund Distinguished Leadership Award.

Dr. Amos Carpenter was a professor of Mathematics and Actuarial Science at Butler University, serving as department head for twelve years. His academic focus included Numerical Analysis, Parallel and Scientific Computing, and the Theory of Computation and Approximation. Carpenter received numerous awards, including the 2008 Distinguished Service Award from the Indiana Section of the Mathematical Association of America.

Eliza Blaker was a pioneer in early childhood development. She helped establish the Indianapolis Free Kindergarten and Children's Aid Society, which became a model for other schools throughout the country. She also founded the Kindergarten Normal Training School, where teachers were taught her methods.

Other "movers and shakers" held sway in the retail industry. Lyman Skinner (L.S.) Ayres began his retail career managing a dry goods business, proving that he understood how to make the shopping experience more pleasurable for his customers. Ayres died during the construction of an eight-story facility, but his son continued his legacy, which became known nationally as L.S. Ayres Department Stores.

Cortland Van Camp formed a partnership with his father in the canning business, but by 1876, Cortland refused to work with perishable foods. Instead, he purchased a hardware company he named Van Camp Hardware and Iron Company. It became the largest hardware business in Indiana during the first half of the twentieth century.

John Francis Geisse, son of aviation pioneer John H. Geisse, founded several successful national department stores, including Target and Venture, and restructured the Ayr-Way store chain. Geisse founded The Wholesale Club, the first membership warehouse store, which was acquired by Sam's Clubs in 1993.

Thomas W. Binford was sports-minded. He implemented safety procedures for the Indy 500 while presiding over the transition from the United States Auto Club (USAC) to the Indy Racing League (IRL). Binford served as Chief Steward of the Indianapolis 500 for twenty-one years and assisted in bringing the Colts professional football team to Indianapolis. He was also a director for both the Automobile Competition Committee of the United States and the Federation Internationale de L'Automobile.

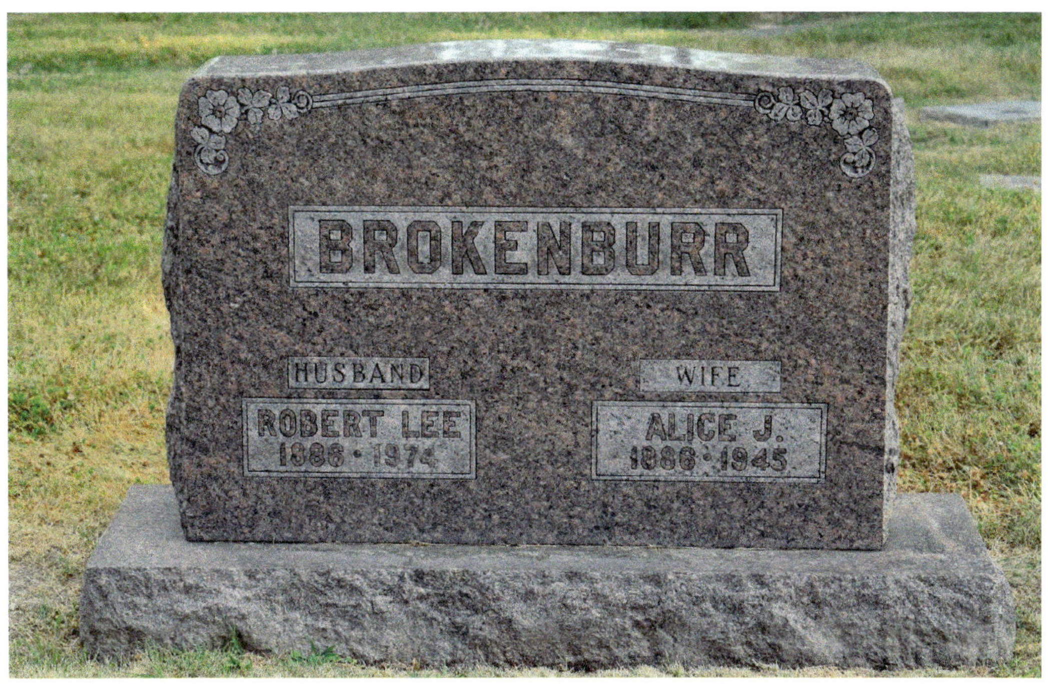

Robert Lee Brokenburr (November 16, 1886 – March 24, 1974) was an African American attorney who brought about change. He became president of the Indianapolis chapter of the NAACP (National Association for the Advancement of Colored People) and was the first African American elected to the Indiana Senate. A red granite headstone marks his grave. (Section 98, Lot 1134) *[Crown Hill Heritage Foundation]*

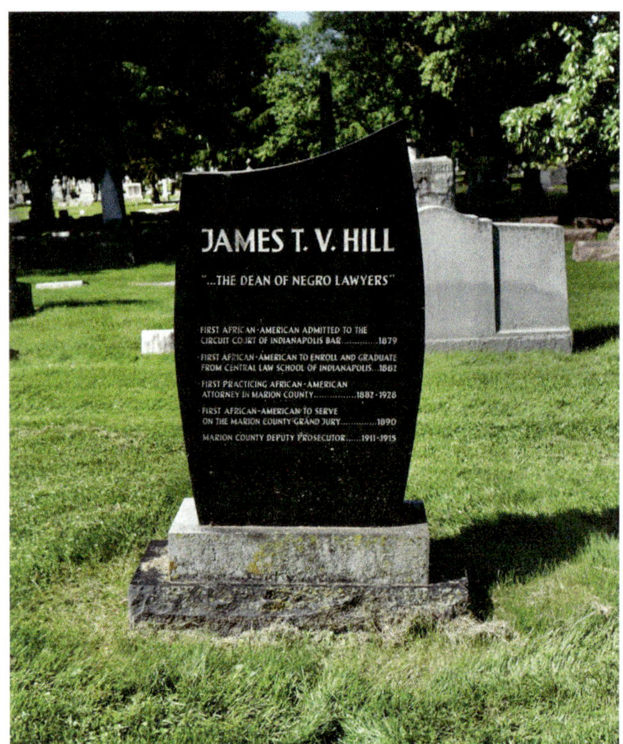

Left: James Thomas Vastine (T. V.) Hill (October 27, 1854 – February 20, 1928) accomplished many "firsts" in Indianapolis. His grave was unmarked until 1998 when the Marion County Bar Association dedicated a polished black granite marker, honoring his numerous achievements. Hill is remembered as " ... the Dean of Negro Lawyers." (Section 35, Lot 160)

Below: Eliza Blaker (March 5, 1854 – December 4, 1926) established the Free Kindergarten Society in Indianapolis, which was later adopted nationwide. Blaker's grave is marked with a small grey granite headstone. (Section 15, Lot 114)

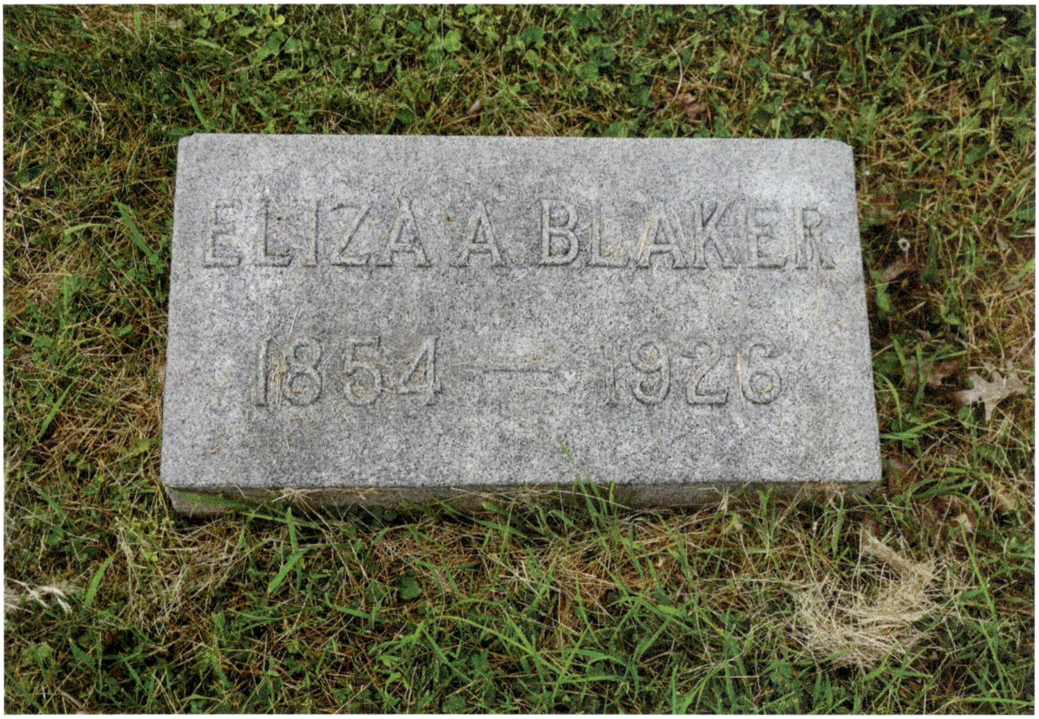

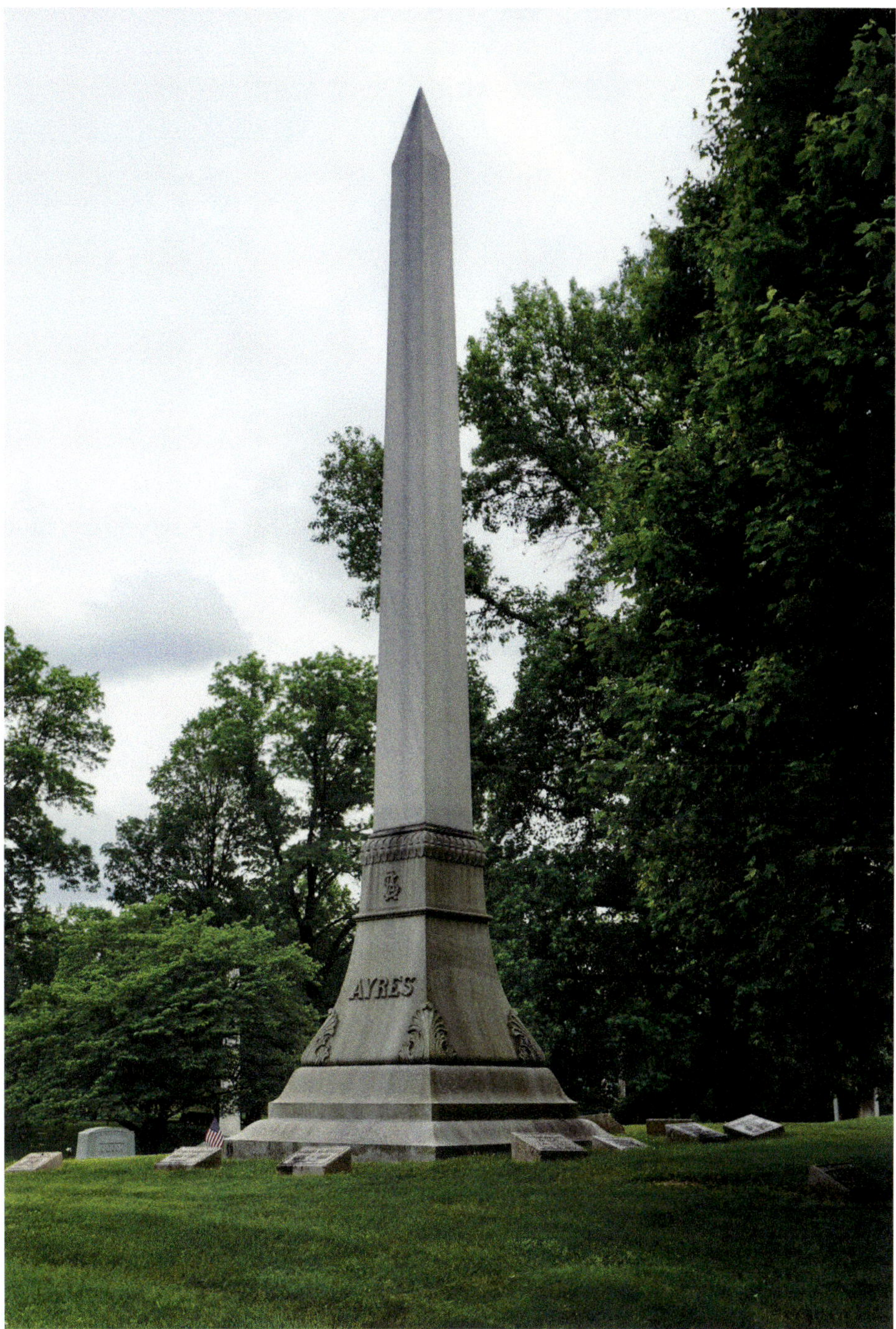

Lyman Skinner (L. S.) Ayres (September 4, 1824 – May 7, 1896) founded the retail store, L.S. Ayres and Company. After Lyman's death, his son developed it nationally into L.S. Ayres Department Stores. The family monument is a soaring granite obelisk with the Ayres name in raised lettering on the front. Family headstones surround the monument. (Section 11, Lot 19)

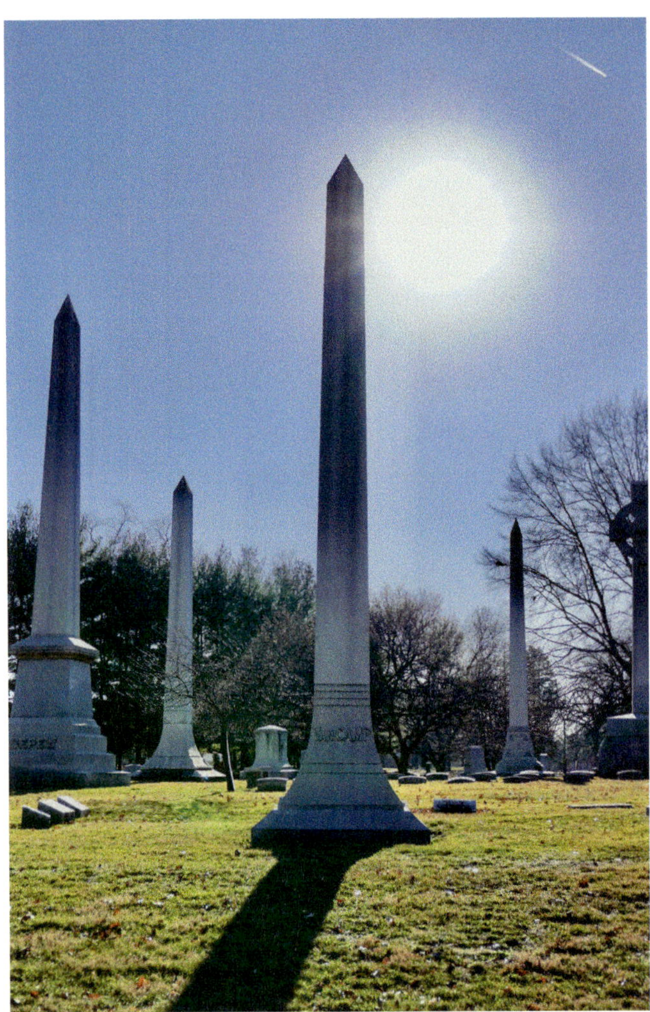

Left: Cortland Van Camp (May 25, 1852 – August 7, 1923) founded the largest hardware business in Indiana. The Van Camp family monument is a tall obelisk built in the Egyptian style. (Section 29, Lot 16)

Below: Thomas W. Binford (April 6, 1924 – January 14, 1999) played a significant role in developing the Indy 500 Speedway and the Indianapolis Colts. Binford's headstone has his motto, "Moral Courage," engraved upon it. A checkered flag plaque stands nearby. (Section 61, Lot 26)

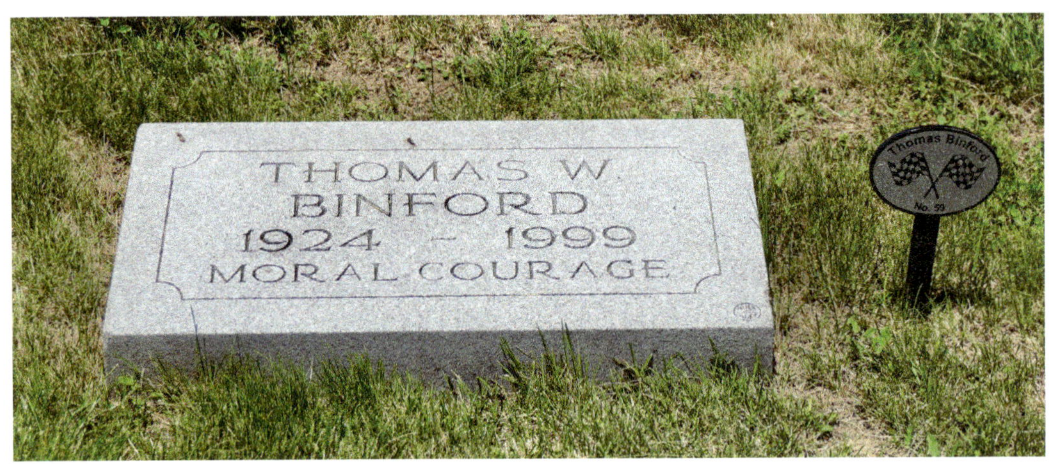

6

Notable People

Notable people make a difference in their community, whether it is in science, engineering, industry, or as activists, humanitarians, and philanthropists. They have the initiative to make their ideas a success, going beyond what a job calls for by putting more of themselves into the role than anyone expected. This is what Indianapolis resident Emma C. Baker did when she answered the call for women to enter the workforce during WWI. Baker was the first African American and the first female to work for the Indianapolis Police Department in 1918. She wore a badge and earned the same pay as male officers. After twenty-one years, she retired as a jail matron. Baker's recent red granite stone has a plaque that tells her story.

Reverend Mozel Sanders was a civil rights activist who marched numerous times with Dr. Martin Luther King, Jr. Sanders founded the first chapter of Opportunities Industrialization Centers, Inc. (OIC), which provided job training to the poor and addicted. Sanders was best known for his Thanksgiving dinners, a tradition that began in 1974, providing local families with traditional holiday dinners. It continues to this day.

Another Indianapolis activist was educator Mattie Rice Coney, who decided to join the fight for civil rights by organizing the Citizen Forum. This grass-roots community program aimed to improve and build better inner-city neighborhoods by encouraging local involvement and self-improvement. The Citizens Forum gained national attention, was recognized, and adopted by several cities in the country.

Cleo Blackburn was an educator and leader who supported numerous civic and educational associations in Indianapolis. He created several self-help programs for veterans before founding the Board for Fundamental Education in 1948, which received a congressional charter in 1954.

Edna Balz Lacy became an Indianapolis businesswoman of high standing, serving as president and board chairman for U.S. Corrugated-Fiber Box Company, which she grew into a national corporation. Lacy was named a Sagamore of the Wabash three times, voted "Woman of the Year" in 1976, and named to the Indiana Business Hall of Fame.

In his spare time, Howard S. Garns created a numbers game. He called it "Number Place." In 1979, it was published by *Dell Pencil Puzzles and Word Games,* but gained little attention. In 1984, *Nikoli Magazine* printed Garns' game under the name "Sudoku," meaning single digit. Garns died in 1989, never aware of how popular his game had become around the world.

Catherine "Hyacinth" Thrash was a member of the Indianapolis-founded religious group, the People's Temple. Group leader Jim Jones moved members to Jonestown, Guyana, where he ordered his congregation to drink cyanide-laced Kool-Aid. Nine-hundred-eighteen people died, but Hyacinth ran into the jungle and escaped, one of only four to make it out alive. Her grave is unmarked.

Herbert "Herbie" Wirth was a beloved door-to-door salesman in Indianapolis who worked six days a week for twenty-five years, and was known for his pleasant attitude and positive outlook. When Herbie died, more than 1,000 people showed up for his graveside services. It was one of the largest memorial services Crown Hill has ever had that was not held for someone "famous."

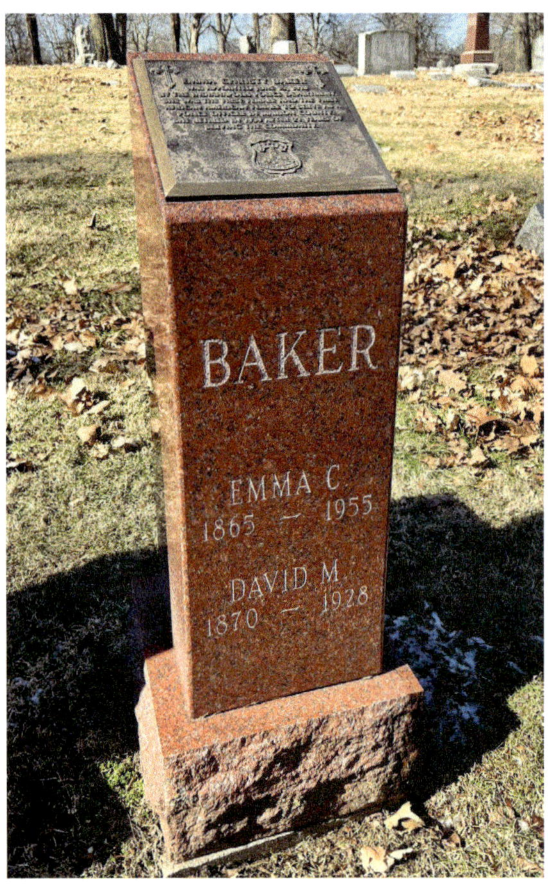

Emma C. Baker (February 10, 1865 – September 23, 1955) was the first African American and the first woman to work for the Indianapolis Police in 1918. Her grave went unmarked until 2003, when an Indianapolis police officer erected the stone with a bronze plaque that tells Baker's story. (Section 37, Lot 82) *[Crown Hill Heritage Foundation]*

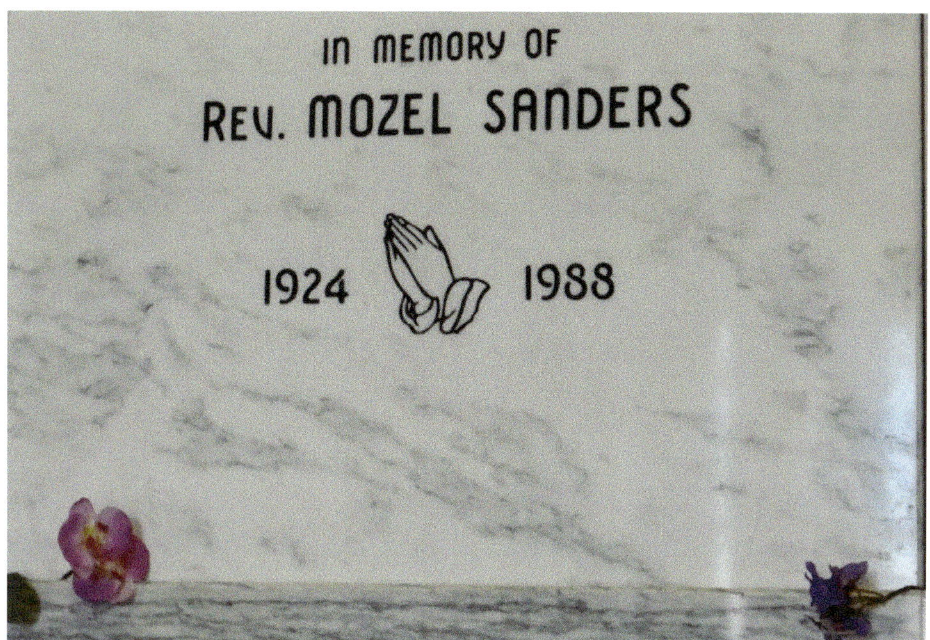

Reverend Mozel Sanders (May 24, 1924 – September 1, 1988) organized community programs to aid those in need. He is best known for providing Thanksgiving dinners for the poor. Praying hands mark his mausoleum crypt. (Community Mausoleum, Corridor 2A, Row D-13)

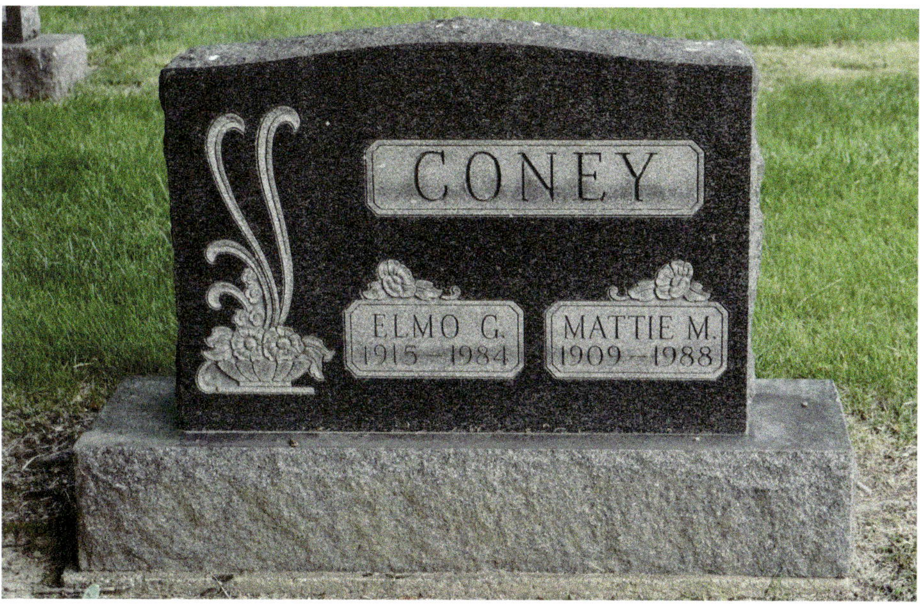

Educator Mattie Rice Coney (May 30, 1909 – August 5, 1988) organized the activist group, Citizens Forum, to improve the lives of residents from inner-city neighborhoods. Her grave is marked with a black granite stone. (Section 46B, Lot 27)

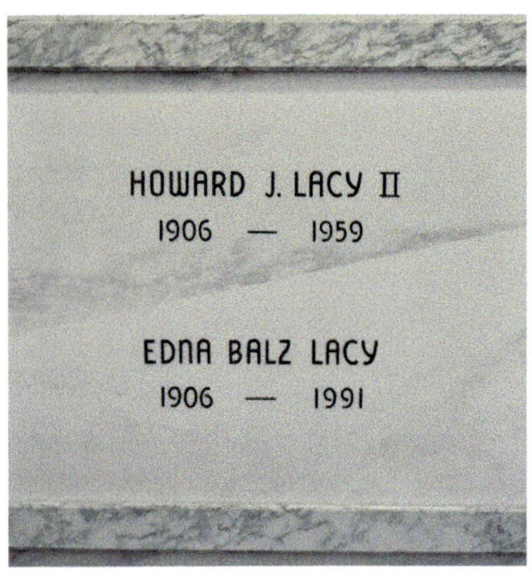

Left: Edna Balz Lacy (September 21, 1906 – December 30, 1991) became president and chair of the board of the U.S. Corrugated-Fiber Box Company when her husband died. Under her leadership, the company grew into a national producer of corrugated boxes. White marble seals her mausoleum crypt. (Community Mausoleum, Corridor C, Row D-6)

Below: Howard Garns (March 2, 1905 – October 6, 1989) created a number puzzle that, when renamed, took the world by storm. Garns died in 1989, never knowing how popular his numbers game, Sudoku, became. (Community Mausoleum (North Building) 2E, Niche E-7))

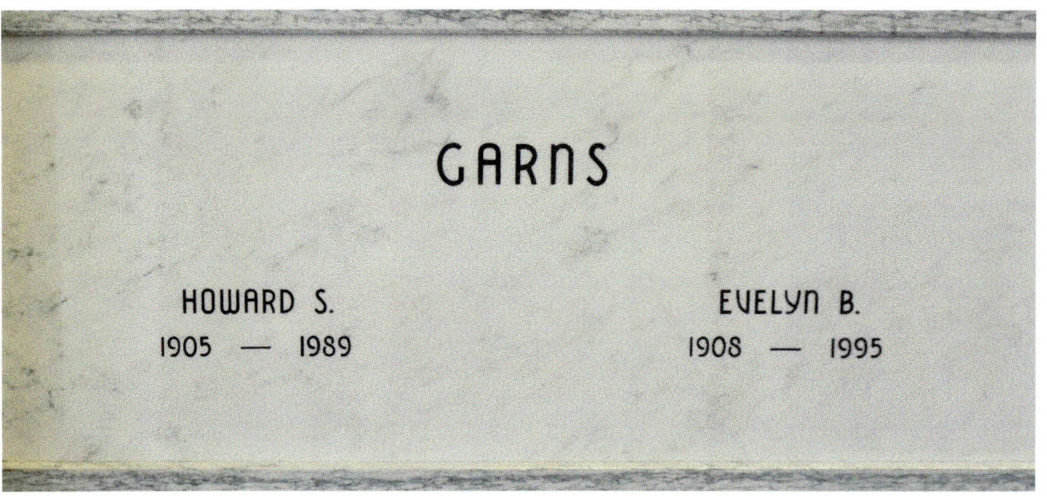

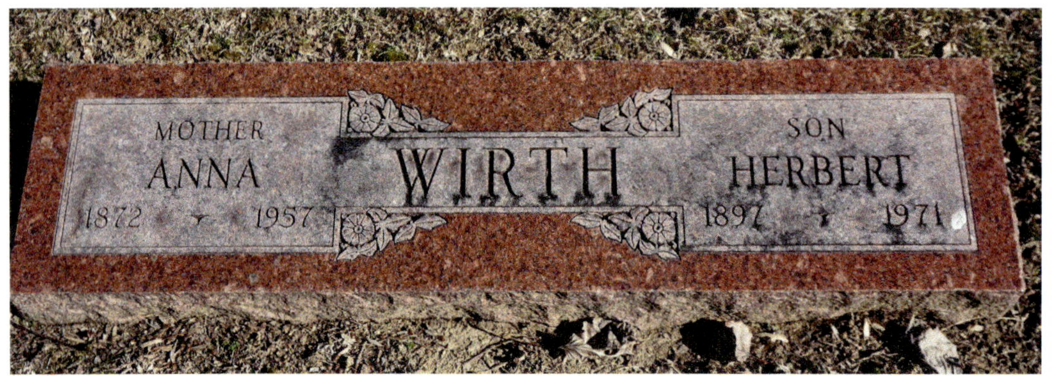

Herbert A. Wirth (June 1897 – January 30, 1971) was a well-loved local door-to-door salesman. More than 1,000 people attended his graveside services, one of the largest attendances held at Crown Hill for someone who was "not famous." (Section 78, Lot 89)

7

The Infamous Souls of Crown Hill

Throughout history, some people became infamous, their names synonymous with scandal, crime, and controversy—those who remind us of the darker aspects of human nature. Whether their actions were driven by greed, power, or malice that shaped their lives and affected the lives of countless others. It is interesting to note that most of the nefarious souls in Crown Hill do not have grave markers, but their stories are interesting.

The most infamous person buried in Crown Hill is John Dillinger, the most famous bank robber of the twentieth century. His gang was responsible for robbing twenty-four banks and four police stations in less than a year, making Dillinger "Public Enemy Number One." He was shot and killed by the FBI outside the Biograph Theatre in Chicago.

Nancy Clem was involved in fraudulent financial operations, which led to the murders of Jacob and Nancy Young in 1868. Known as the Cold Spring Murders, Clem was accused of setting up the killings. She was tried four times, with the final trial resulting in a life prison sentence, but the Supreme Court pardoned her in 1874.

John H. Achey and his younger brother, David, were in trouble with the law their entire lives. David Achey provoked a fight in front of an Indianapolis saloon and was shot to death in June 1868. Brother John was playing pool when he accused George Leggett of cheating him out of $875. Achey shot Leggett and was tried and convicted of the murder. Achey made a name for himself as the first person to be hanged in Indianapolis.

Clarence H. Euell was an African American waiter at the English Hotel in 1917, when Dan Shay, manager of the Milwaukee Brewers baseball team, made a racist comment to him. Shay then pulled a revolver and shot Euell in the stomach. Despite being mortally injured, Euell wrestled Shay down and beat his head on the floor. Euell was rushed to the hospital, where he died. Shay was acquitted of second-degree murder by an all-white jury.

Heiress and widow Marjorie Jackson was murdered during a burglary at her home in 1977. After her husband died, she began keeping his nine-million-dollar fortune hidden in the house. One night, two men broke into the home and shot her before setting fire to the house. Jackson died in the blaze. Both men were convicted of murder and the largest cash robbery in the United States.

Forrest Teel had it all: vice president of marketing for Eli Lilly Company, wealthy with an impressive home, and a jealous mistress. But one night, Teel was gunned down, and his mistress, Minnie B. (Connie) Nicholas, was charged. She claimed the shooting was accidental after an argument about Teel's "new girlfriend." Nicholas was convicted of voluntary manslaughter but served only two years before being released and disappearing from Indianapolis.

The scandal of grave robbing rocked Indianapolis in 1902 when five doctors were indicted along with a "Gang of Ghouls." Dr. Joseph Alexander, an Indianapolis physician and director of the anatomical laboratory at Central College of Physicians and Surgeons, was arrested and charged with disturbing a grave, taking a corpse, and aiding in the concealment of a dead body. His trial ended in a hung jury, and charges were dropped in 1903. Alexander's grave remains unmarked.

Another well-known grave robber of the time was Wade Hampton West, a member of the "Gang of Ghouls" who helped steal bodies from the cemetery to sell to medical schools. West was arrested and died in prison.

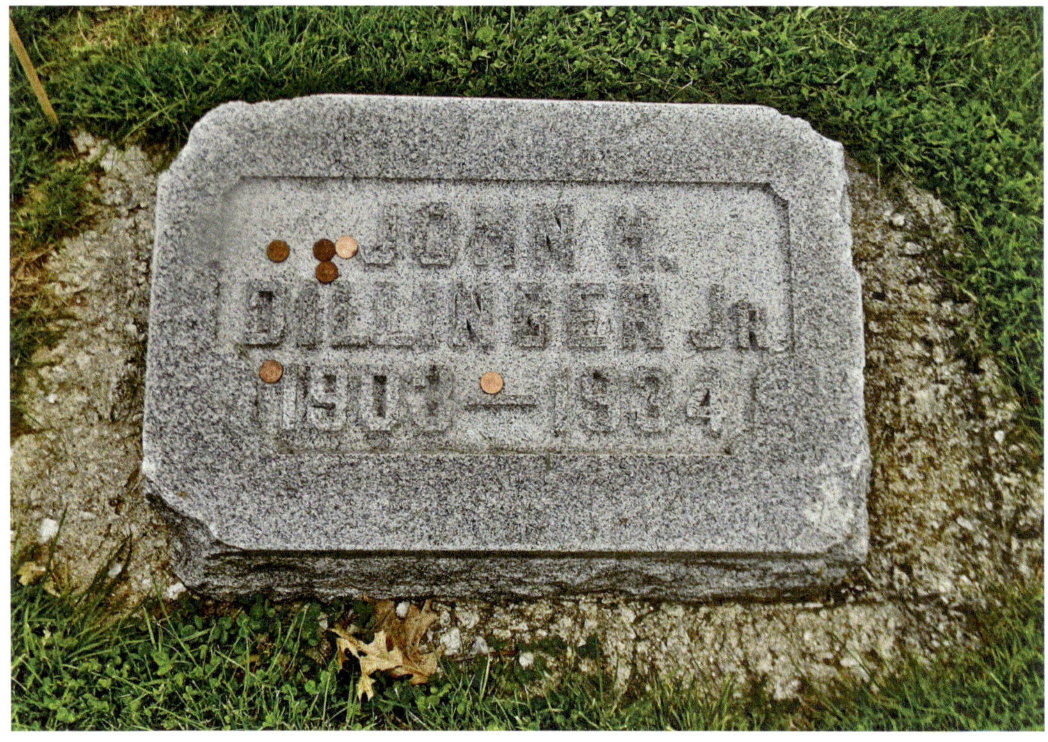

John Herbert Dillinger, Jr. (June 22, 1903 – July 22, 1934) became one of America's most famous criminals during the Great Depression. His stone is one of the most visited in the cemetery, with coins and flowers left as gifts. Notice the marker's edges are broken where people have chipped off pieces as souvenirs. (Section 44, Lot 94)

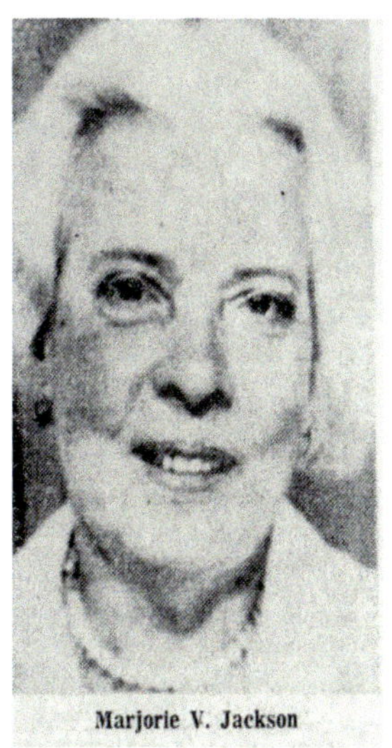
Marjorie V. Jackson

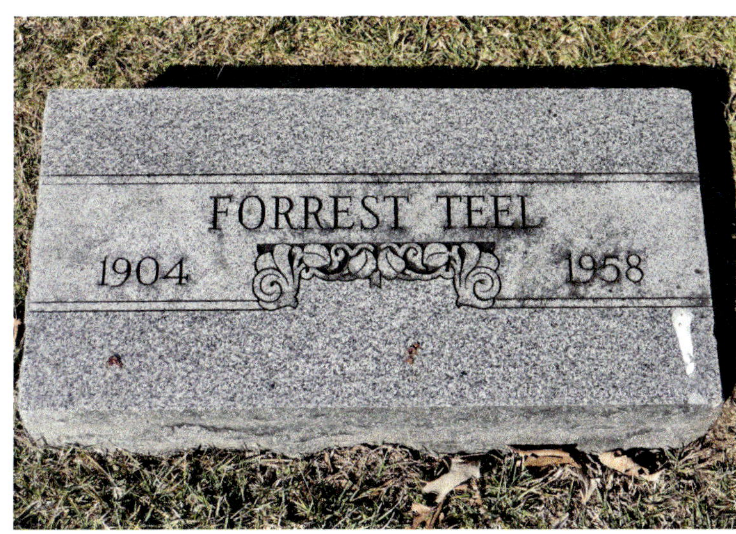

Above left: Marjorie Viola O'Connell Jackson (November 30, 1910 – May 5, 1977) was an eccentric Indianapolis millionaire murdered during a home robbery in 1977. Her killers were caught and convicted of the largest cash robbery in the U.S. (Section 55, Lot 244) *[Newspapers.com, Indianapolis News]*

Above right: Forrest Teel (May 24, 1904 – July 31, 1958) was a prominent executive at Eli Lilly Company when he was shot to death by his lover, Connie Nicholas, during an argument in his car. The case was so scandalous that it became one of the most publicized trials in Indianapolis' history. A small headstone marks Teel's grave. (Section 212, Lot 883)

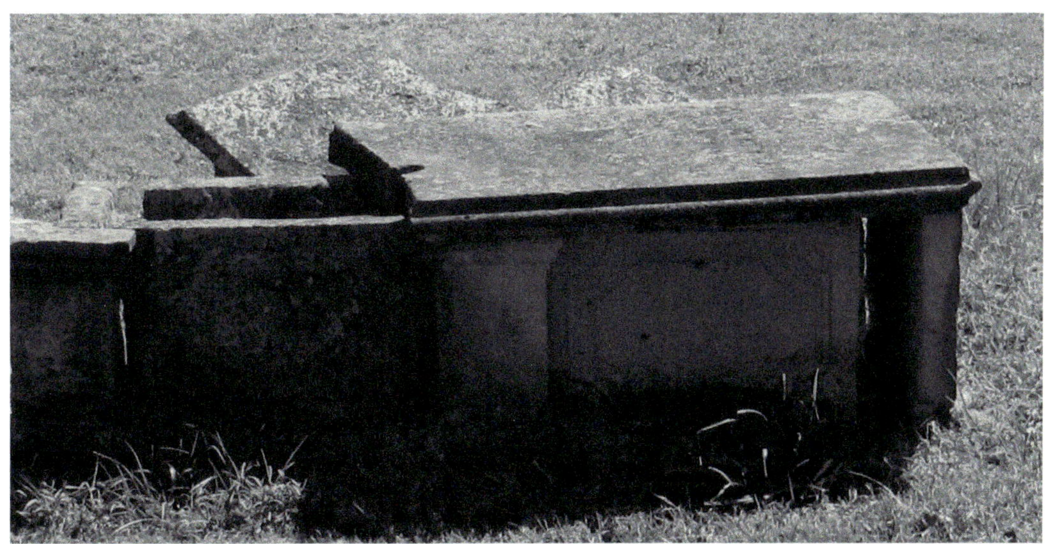

Dr. Joseph C. Alexander was infamously implicated in a grave-robbing scandal. He was arrested, but his trial ended in a hung jury. Alexander's grave remains unmarked, possibly to thwart graverobbers.

8

The Politicians of Crown Hill

The early nineteenth century's political climate was heavily influenced by transportation routes that ran through the state, with Indianapolis as the center of activity. The Civil War tested the Hoosier State's loyalty to the Union and brought about a more diverse population as residents embraced Republican ethics.

At the turn of the twentieth century, politics moved toward a more progressive attitude. But with the Great Depression's New Deal and the post-World War II boom, the state saw more opportunities become available for its citizens through the Democratic Party. Civil Rights, urban renewal, and economic development established the political movement that has led to more civic and diverse set of opinions in the twenty-first century.

Crown Hill has scores of politicians at rest, including one U.S. president and first lady, four vice presidents, eleven governors, fourteen congressmen, three U.S. senators, and numerous state and local officials.

The only president buried at Crown Hill is Benjamin Harrison, who served as America's twenty-third president from 1889 to 1893. His family included a signer of the Declaration of Independence, and the ninth U.S. president, William Henry Harrison. During his term, Harrison expanded and modernized the U.S. Navy, signed into existence three national parks, oversaw six new states join the country, and supervised the nation's first billion-dollar budget.

Three vice presidents rest at Crown Hill. Former Indiana governor and twenty-first Vice President, Thomas A. Hendricks, served with President Grover Cleveland. Hendricks' funeral was the first to enter through the ornate Gothic Gates. Twenty-sixth Vice President Charles Fairbanks served under President Theodore Roosevelt. The Alaskan town of Fairbanks was named in his honor. Twenty-eighth Vice President Thomas Marshall served for two terms under President Woodrow Wilson. During 1919, Marshall acted in numerous ceremonial roles as Wilson recovered from a stroke.

There are eleven governors buried at Crown Home. Among those are Governor Oliver Morton, who served as the fourteenth Indiana governor, and the first to be buried at Crown Hill. Governor Ira J. Chase served as lieutenant governor and then the twenty-second governor of Indiana. During his term, Chase approved the Soldiers and Sailors Monument in Indianapolis and improved the Indiana road system. The twenty-fifth governor was Winfred Durbin, who served one term. Governor Robert Orr became governor in 1980 and served two terms. He was appointed Ambassador to Singapore by President George W. Bush, a position he held until 1992.

Secretary of State Larry Conrad served as Senator Birch Bayh's legislative assistant. When Bayh was seriously injured in a plane crash, Conrad steered the Twenty-fifth Amendment, which documents the line of succession if the president is killed or incapacitated, through committees to Congressional approval and ratification. Conrad also served as Secretary of State.

Caleb Blood Smith served as President Abraham Lincoln's Secretary of the Interior. When Smith died, his wife refused to say where he was buried due to threats from Southern sympathizers to dig up his body.

U.S. Representative William Eastin English served in the U.S. House of Representatives and the Indiana Senate. He served as vice president of the National Association of Democratic Clubs before switching to the Republican Party. Indiana State Senator Arcada Stark Balz was the first woman elected to the Indiana Senate in 1942 and served until 1950. She chaired the Senate Committee on Public Health in 1947.

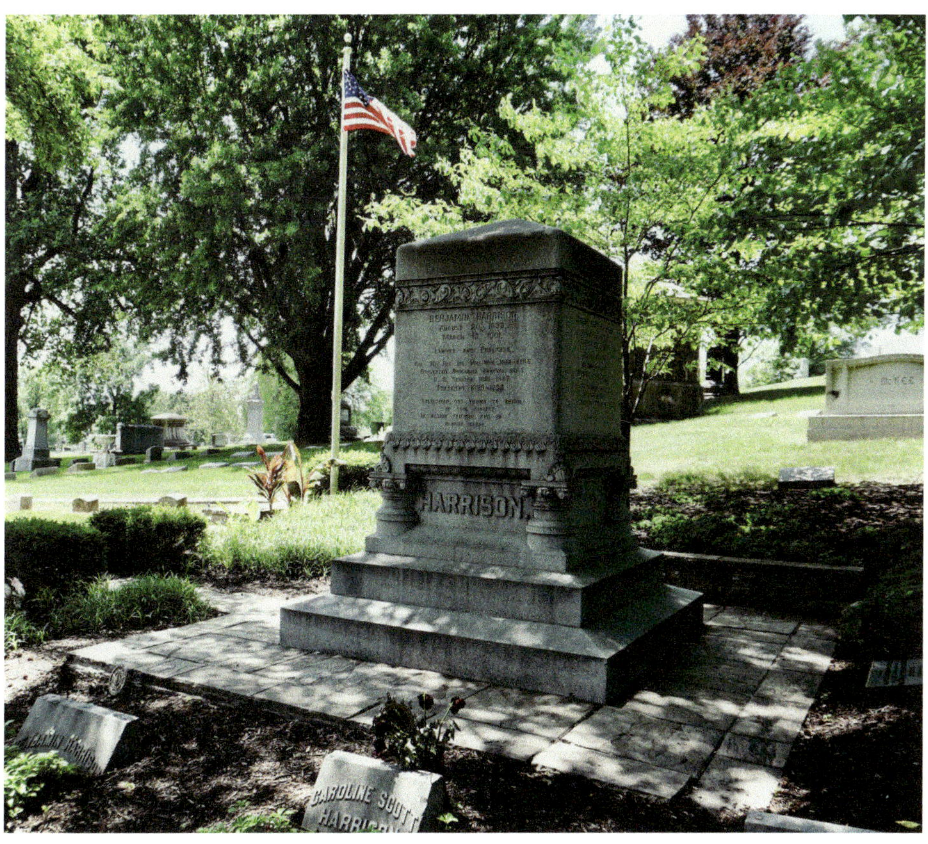

The Benjamin Harrison family stone features the classical details of a footed chest raised on a three-step base. Besides serving as president, Harrison's monument notes he was a "statesman, yet friend to truth, of soul sincere. In action faithful, and in honor clear." (Section 13, Lot 57)

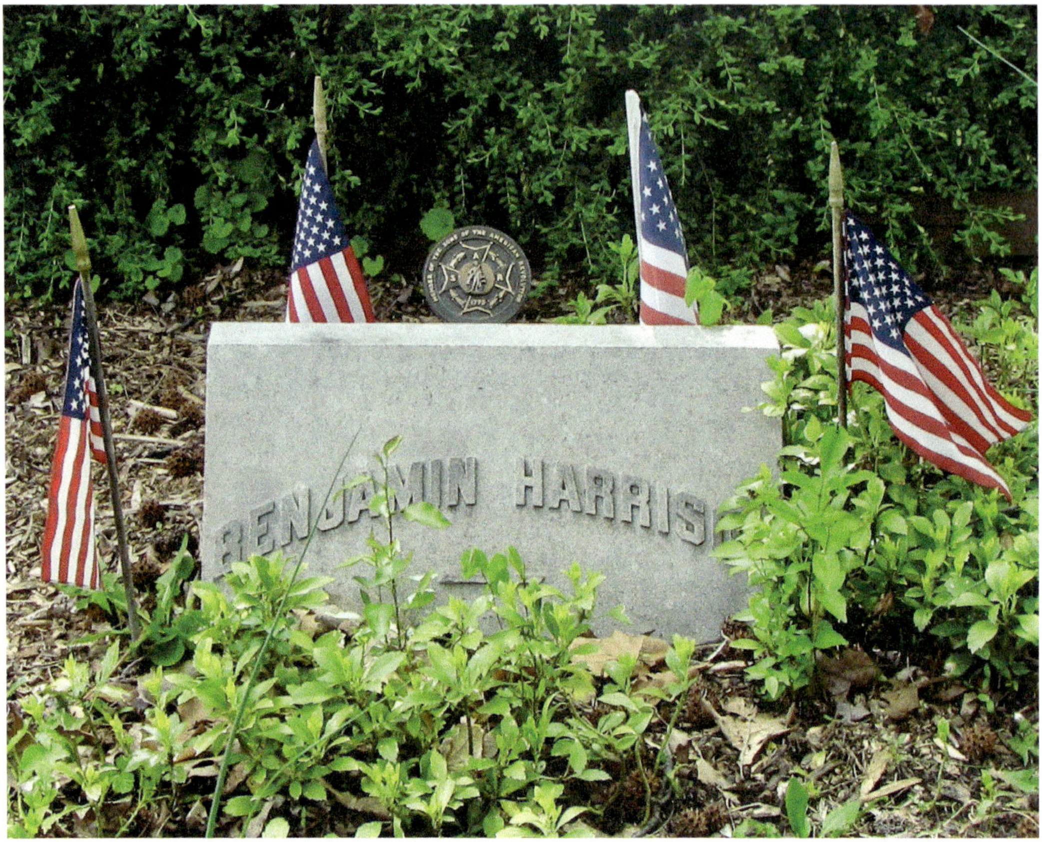

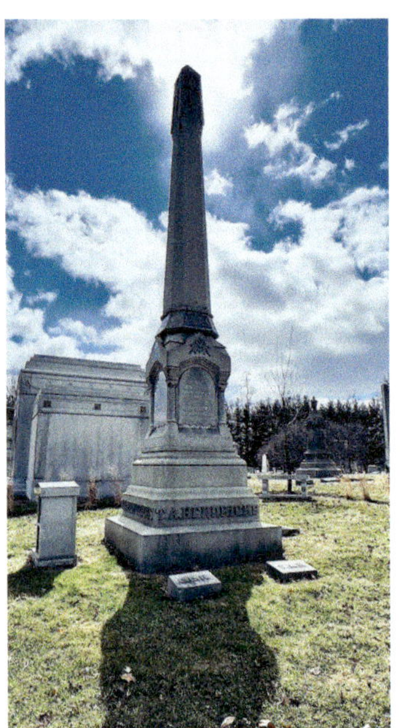

Above: President Benjamin Harrison (August 20, 1833 – March 13, 1901), twenty-third president of the United States, has a granite headstone marking his grave.

Left: Vice President Thomas Andrew Hendricks (September 7, 1819 – November 25, 1885) served under President Grover Cleveland. Hendricks also served in the U.S. House of Representatives, the U.S. Senate, and was commissioner of the U.S. General Land Office. His grave is marked with a tall, granite obelisk, and his funeral was the first to enter through the new Gothic Gates. (Section 29, Lot 2) [*Marcus Collins*]

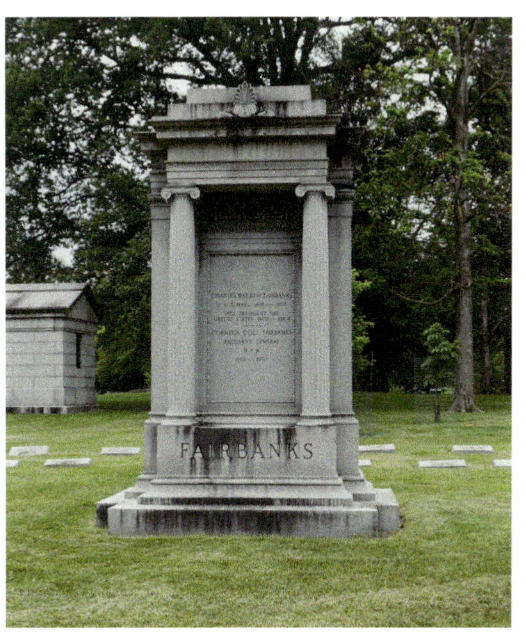

Right: Vice President Charles Fairbanks (May 11, 1852 – June 4, 1918) served under President Theodore Roosevelt. In 1901, Fairbanks became the leader of the U.S. Senate and the Republican National Committee. His monument features Doric-style columns and embellishments. Section 24, Lot 3)

Below: Vice President Thomas R. Marshall (March 14, 1854 – June 1, 1925) was elected governor of Indiana in 1908 and served two terms as vice president with President Woodrow Wilson. Marshall's mausoleum is a classic design with closed urns on either side of the bronze and glass doors. (Section 72, Lot 1)

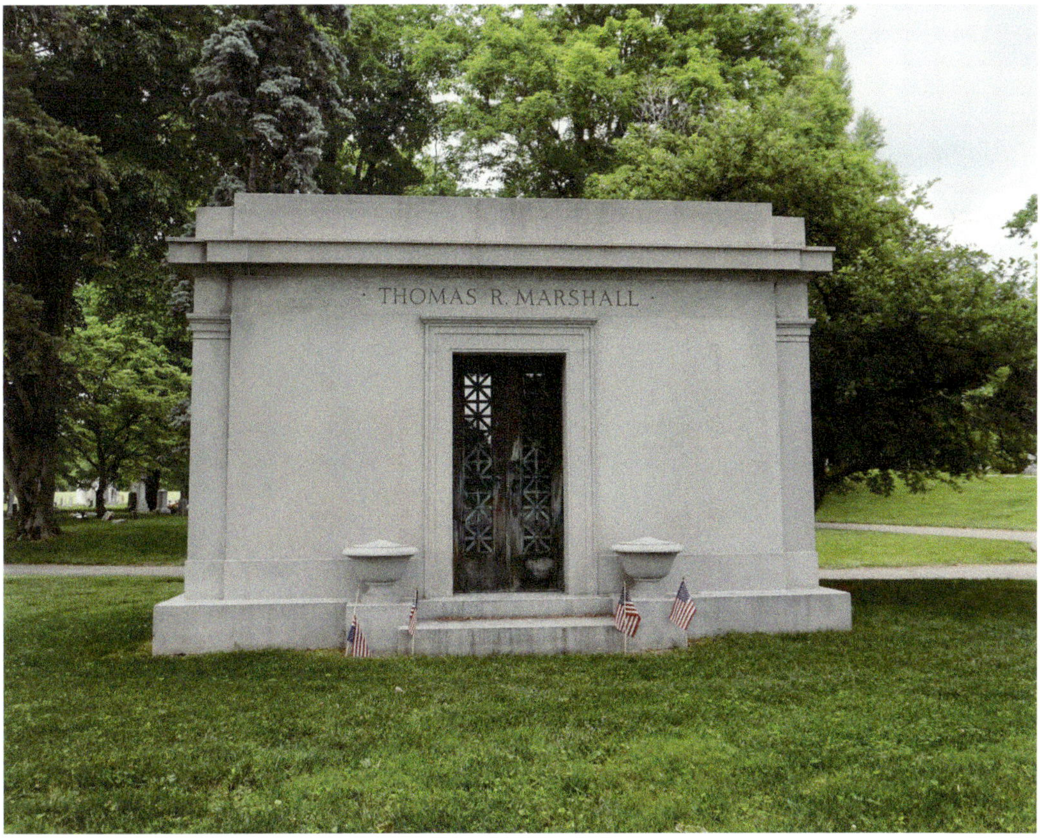

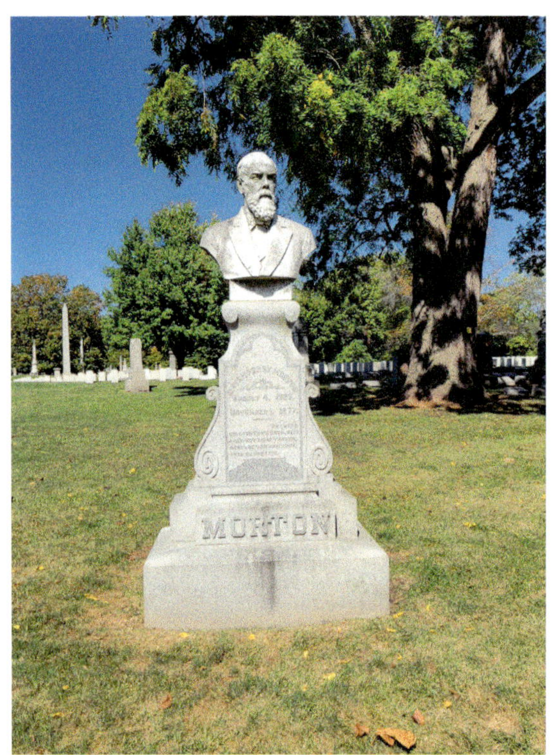

Left: Governor Oliver Perry Morton (August 4, 1823 – November 1, 1877) served as the fourteenth governor and was a fierce supporter of President Abraham Lincoln and the Union. He was then elected to serve two terms in the U.S. Senate, where he died in 1877. Morton was the first governor buried at Crown Hill, and his monument and bust are done in a classical style. (Section 9, Lot 37)

Below: Governor Ira Joy Chase (December 7, 1834 – May 11, 1895) served as lieutenant governor of Indiana. He was appointed to serve as the twenty-second governor after the death of Governor Alvin Hovey. His grave is marked with a simple headstone. (Section 9, Lot 39)

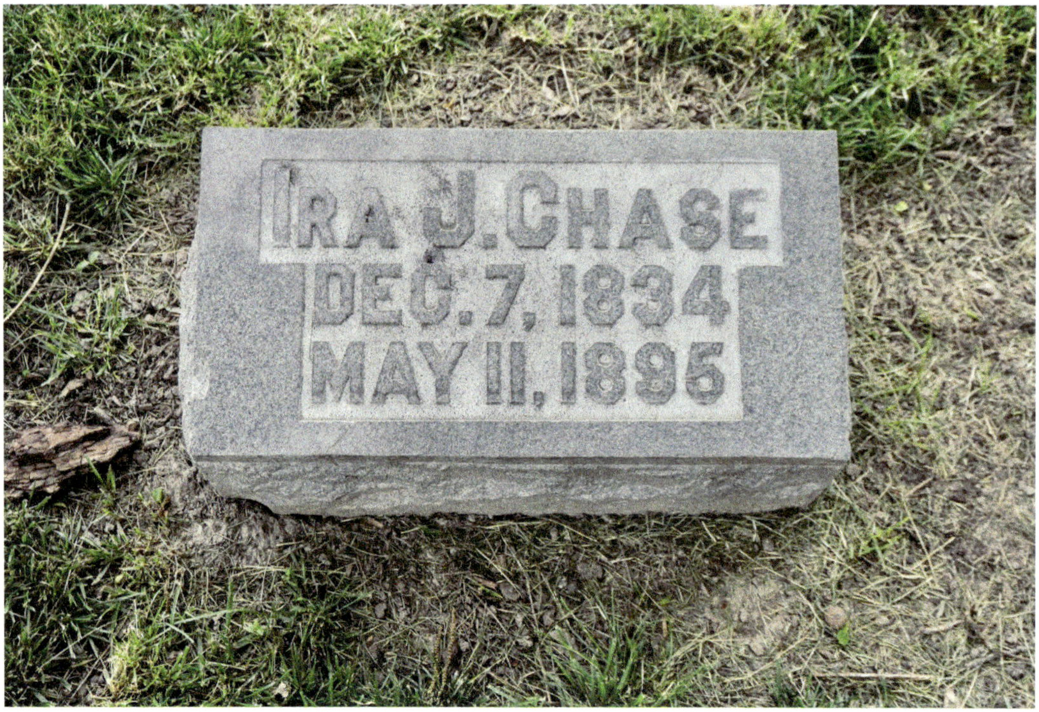

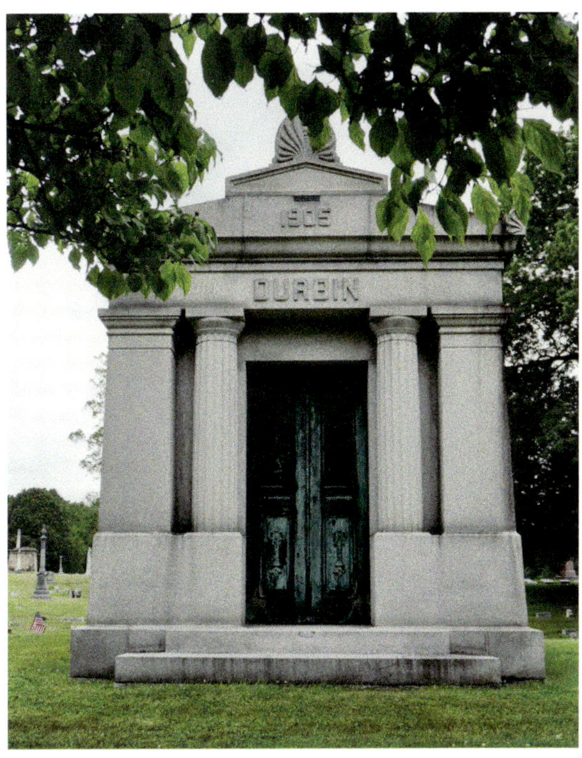

Right: Governor Winfield Taylor Durbin (May 4, 1847 – December 18, 1928) was chairman of the Republican State Executive Committee for six years before being elected the twenty-fifth governor of Indiana. At the entrance of Durbin's mausoleum, square and classical pillars surround the bronze double doors, which bear two upside-down torches of life about to be extinguished. (Section 23, Lot 11)

Below: Governor Robert Orr (November 17, 1917 – March 10, 2004) was elected to the Indiana Senate in 1968. He served two terms as lieutenant governor under Otis R. Bowen. Orr became governor in 1980 and served another two terms. A curved granite bench marks his and his wife's graves. (Section 24, Lot 63)

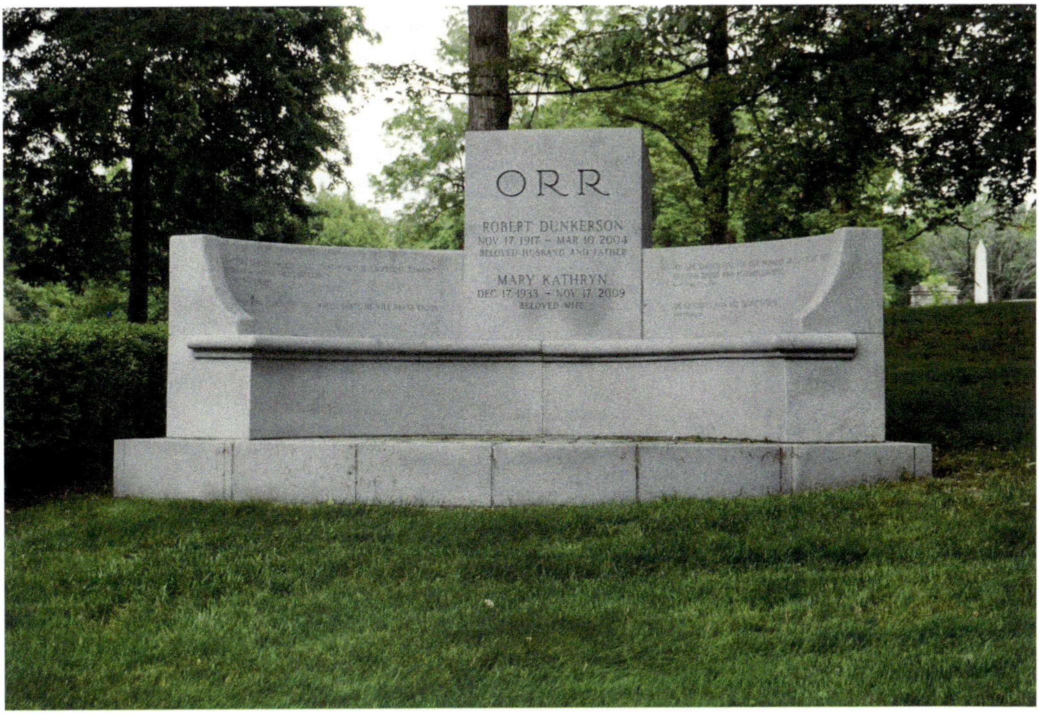

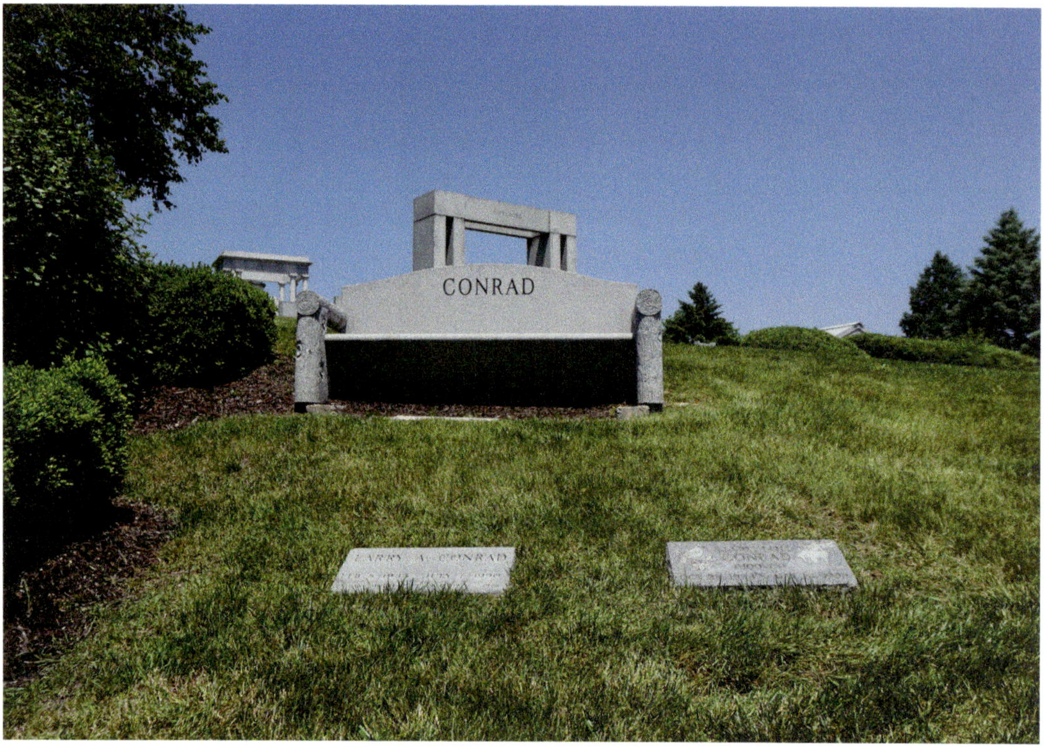

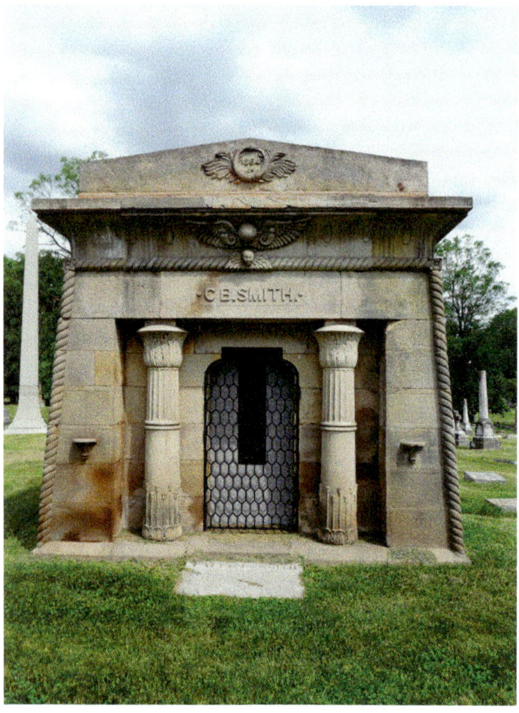

Above: Secretary of State Larry Conrad (February 8, 1935-July 7, 1990) was Indiana Secretary of State from 1970 to 1978. He was instrumental in getting the Congressional passage of the Twenty-fifth Amendment. The family bench is decorated with rugged tree-stone arms and legs. (Section 88, Lot 14)

Left: Secretary of the Interior, Caleb Blood Smith (April 16, 1808 – January 7, 1864) served as a Whig in the Indiana House of Representatives and U.S. House of Representatives. The exact location of his grave is not known due to threats from southerners to "dig his body up." (Section 5, Lot 9 Smith Family Mausoleum)

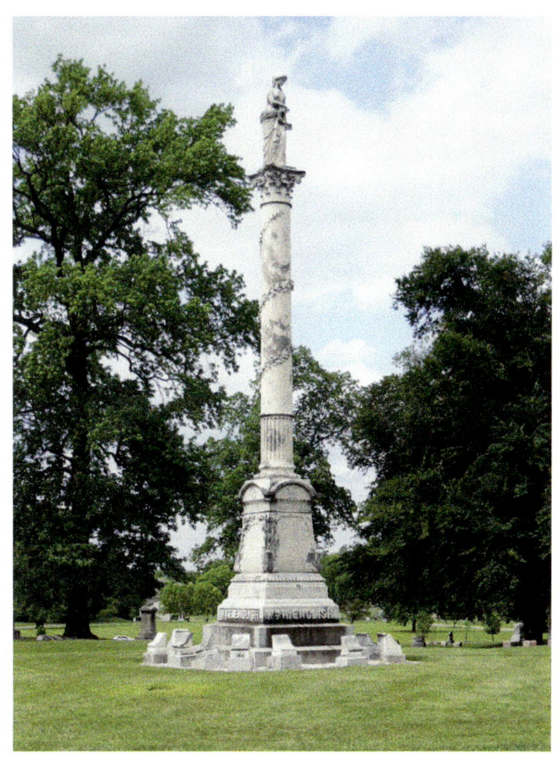

Right: Congressman William English (November 3, 1850 – April 29, 1926) served two terms in the Indiana House of Representatives and one term in the Indiana Senate. The classical column high atop his monument is wrapped with ivy for remembrance as it soars skyward. A mourning woman stands atop, holding the wreath of victory over death. (Section 1, Lot 72)

Below: Indiana State Senator Arcada Stark Balz (December 28, 1879 – August 18, 1973) served as the first woman elected to the Indian Senate and the first female chair of the Senate Committee on Public Health. (Section 3, Lot 91)

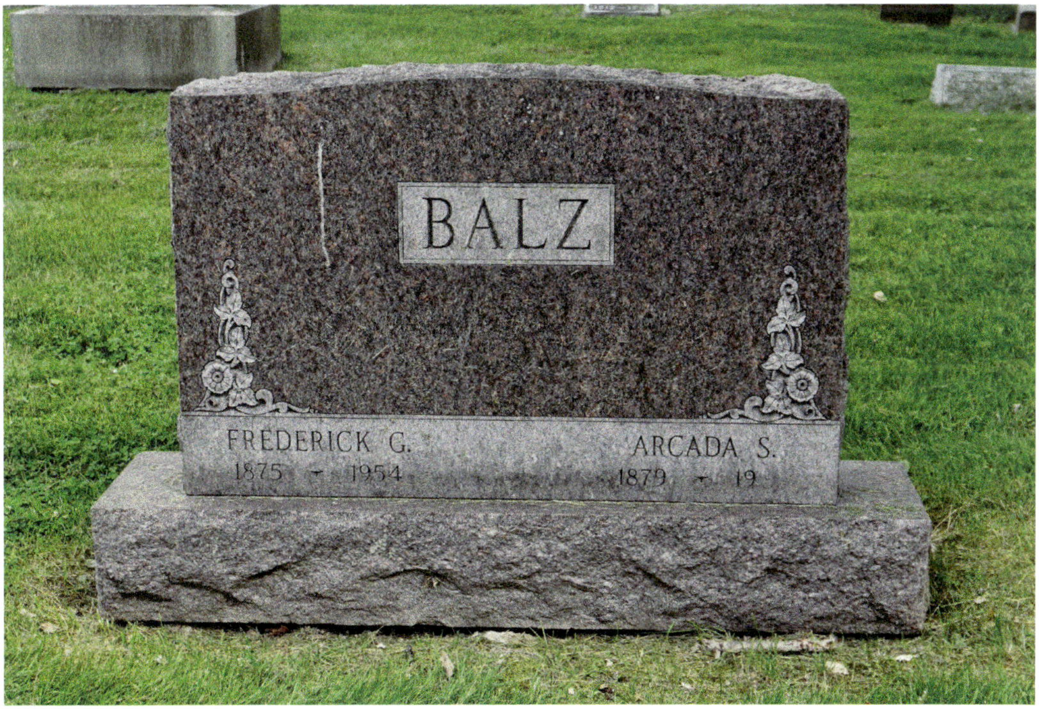

9

Suffragettes of the Cemetery

Hoosier women played a significant role in the state and national suffrage movements. Indiana women used "petticoat diplomacy" by setting up booths at county fairs, circulating petitions, and making speeches to advocate for equal rights. Hoosier Amanda Way was known as the "Mother of Women's Suffrage in Indiana." She organized the first Women's Rights Convention in Dublin, Indiana, in 1851.

May Wright Sewall founded the Indianapolis Equal Suffrage Society. She was also president of the National Council of Women of the United States and president of the International Council. Sewall died one month before the passage of the Nineteenth Amendment, which gave women the right to vote. Julia E. Landers played an integral part in the national and Indiana suffrage movements. She served as chairman of the executive committee of the National Suffrage Association, president of the National Council of Women of the United States, president of the International Council, and as the first Hoosier elected as Democratic National Chairwoman. She helped organize the League of Women Voters and assisted in passing the Nineteenth Amendment.

Zerelda Gray Sanders Wallace served as first lady of Indiana from 1837 to 1840 during the governorship of her husband, David Wallace. She was the first president of the Women's Christian Temperance Union and served as vice president of the National Woman Suffrage Association serving with Susan B. Anthony. Dr. Amelia R. Keller was one of the first female doctors in Indianapolis and the first president of the Woman's Franchise League of Indiana. Keller was also the first woman to receive a paid faculty position at Indiana University School of Medicine. She assisted in getting the Nineteenth Amendment ratified.

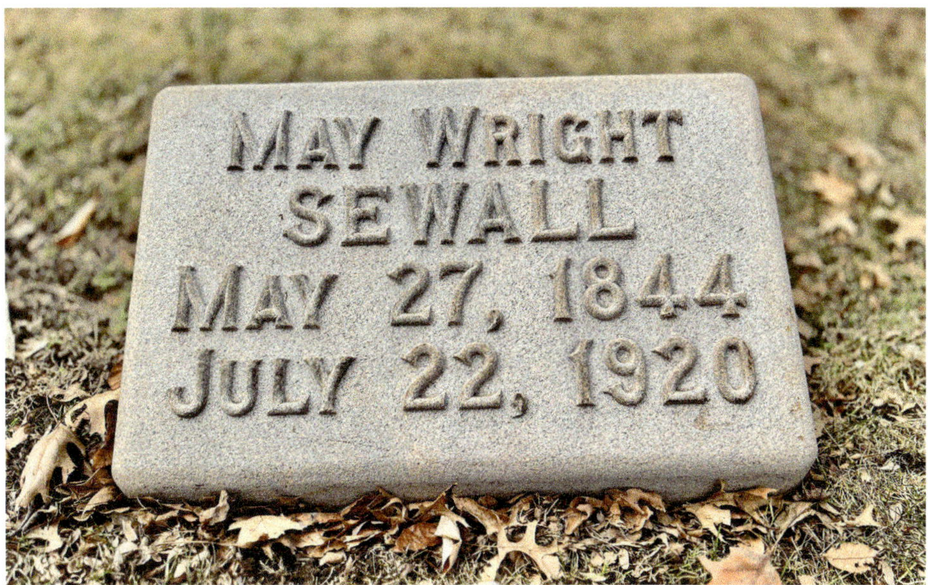

May Wright Sewall (May 27, 1844 – July 22, 1920) served as chairman of the executive committee of the National Suffrage Association. Sewall died one month before the passage of the Nineteenth Amendment, which gave women the right to vote. A plain headstone marks her grave. (Section 13, Lot 24) *[Marcus Collins]*

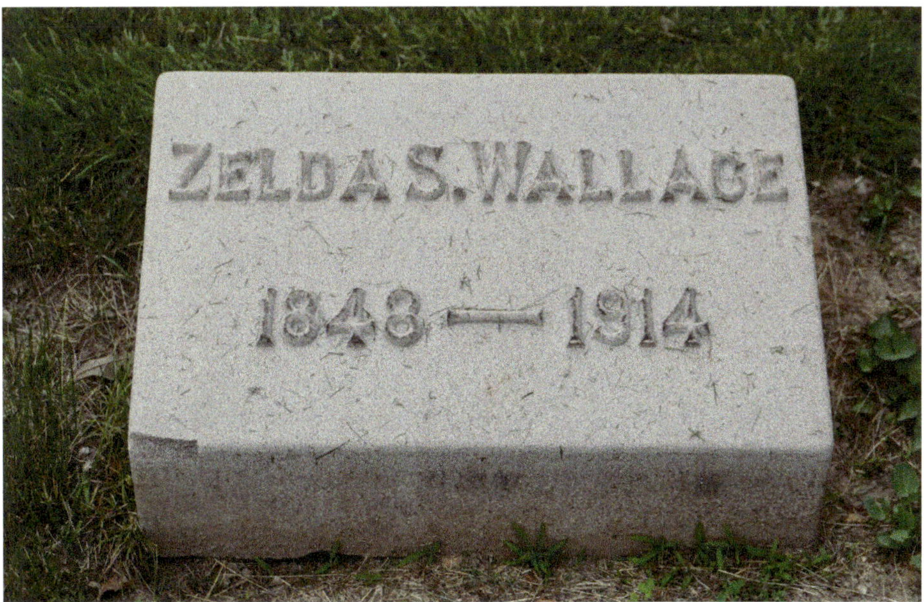

Zerelda Gray Sanders Wallace (August 6, 1817 – March 19, 1901) was a temperance activist, suffragist leader, and a motivational speaker for both organizations. Wallace's grave is marked with a plain headstone. Notice that her first name has been abbreviated to Zelda. (Section 3, Lot 10)

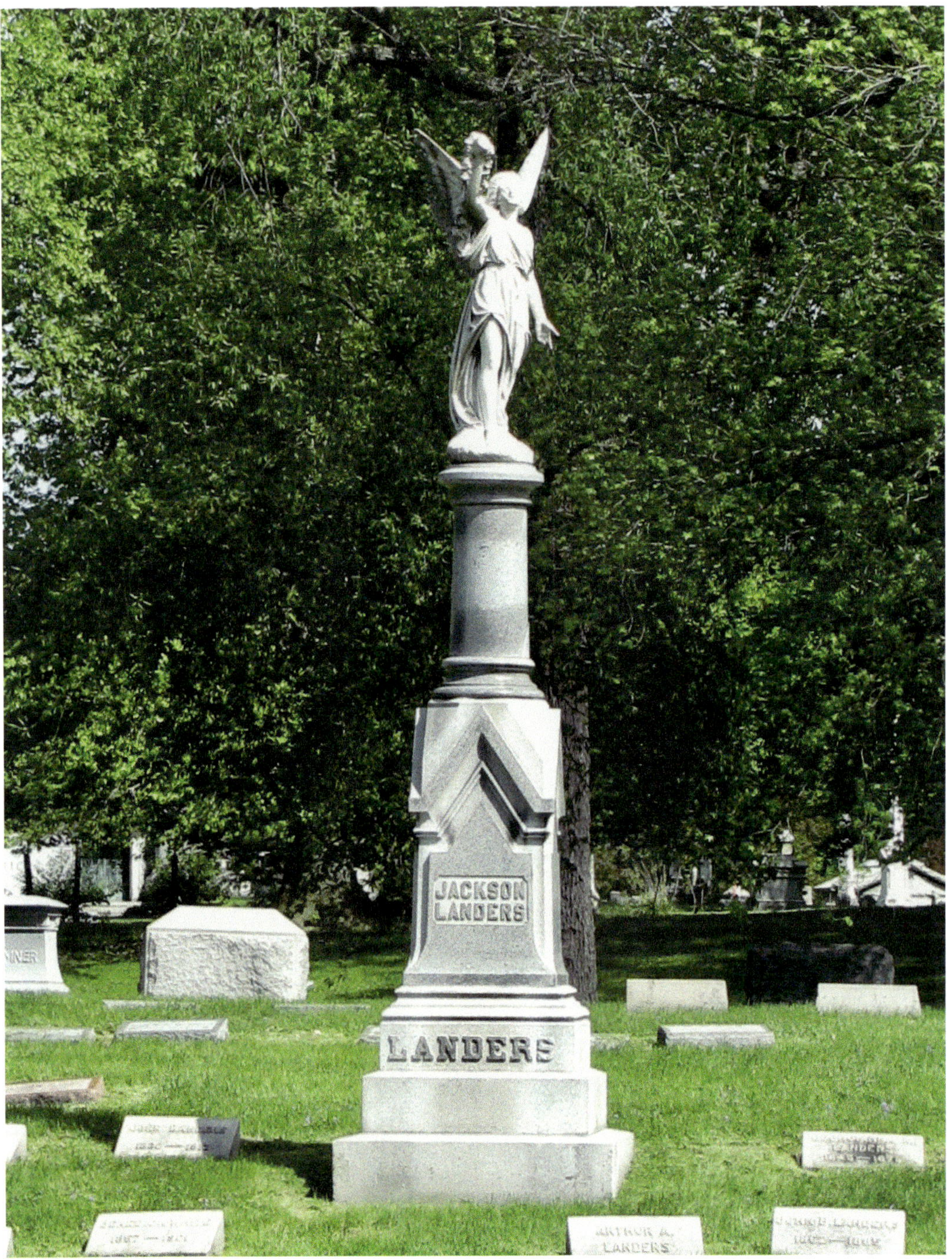

Julia E. Landers (June 19, 1874 – April 12, 1953) was the first woman to serve on an election board. She also helped organize the League of Women Voters and assisted in passing the Nineteenth Amendment. An angel scatters the petals of life from atop Landers' monument. (Section 12, Lot 28)

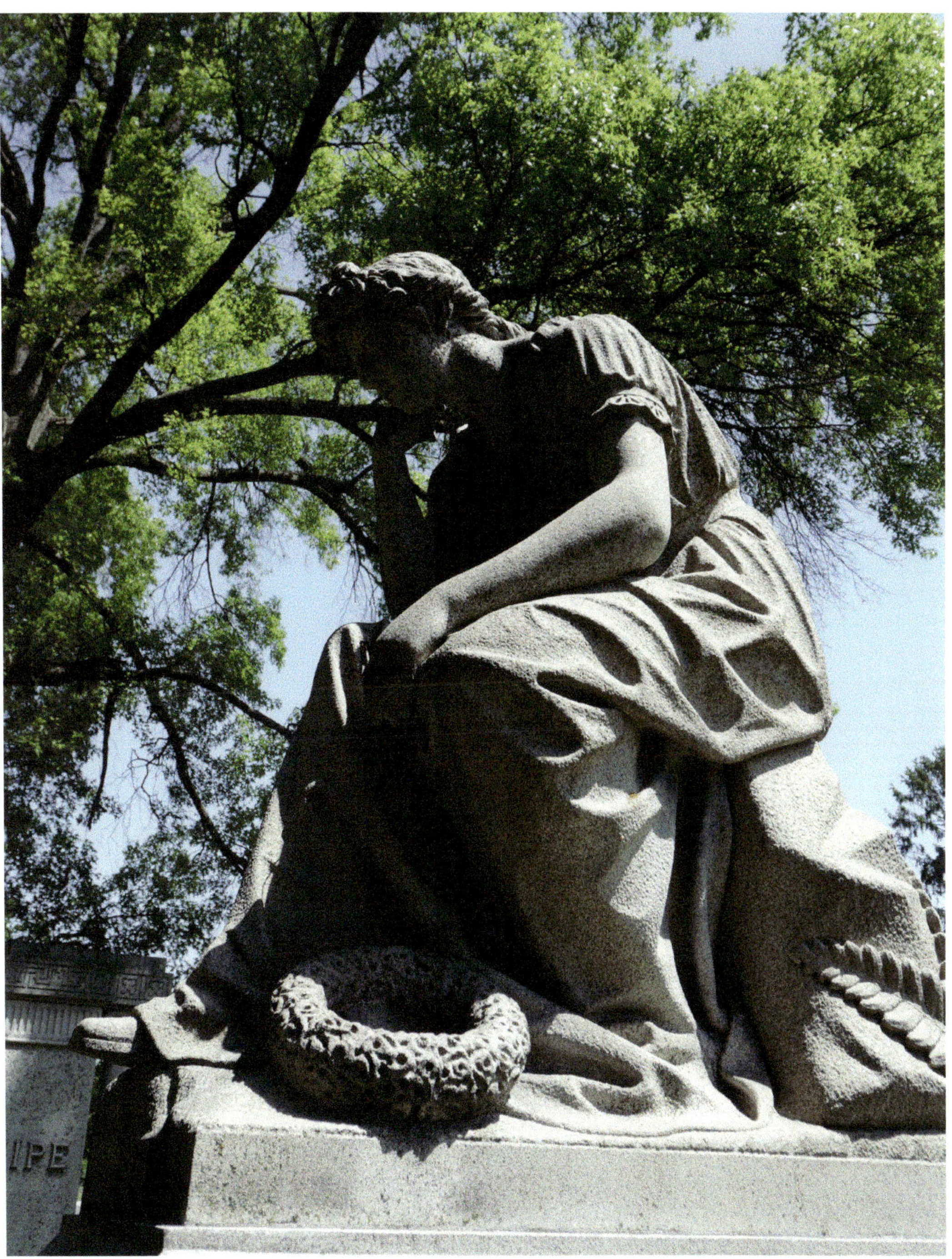

Dr. Amelia R. Keller (January 12, 1871 – January 28, 1943) was one of the first female physicians in the city and had a significant role in ratifying the Nineteenth Amendment. A woman sits in deep contemplation atop her monument with the wreath of victory over death at her feet. (Section 58, Lot 34)

10

Artists, Writers, and Performers at Crown Hill

Indiana has a rich cultural history. It has been the home of well-loved authors and writers, vibrant artists, and numerous performers. Thanks to dedicated art patrons, and several literary and artistic institutions, Indianapolis is a haven for artistic Hoosiers.

Artist John Washington Love was the first Hoosier to attend École des Beaux-Arts, the oldest and most prestigious art school in France. Love, and artist James Farrington Gookins, co-founded the Indiana School of Art, the first professional art school in the state. Landscape artist Mabel Dorothy Morlan was mentored by Hoosier Group artists J. Otis Adams and William Forsyth. She was one of sixteen artists who painted two landscape murals for the Indianapolis City Hospital wards. Lucy Martha Taggart was well-known for her portraiture work. Her paintings were shown at the Pennsylvania Academy of Fine Arts and the National Association of Women Painters and Sculptors. Herman Lieber ran a stationery and bookbinding store where he befriended local artists. Lieber became a patron of the arts and supported several Indiana painters, including T. C. Steele.

Sculptor Jeffrey Lawrence Bratton was an artist and teacher who designed his monument before his death at the age of twenty-three. His monument is designated as one of Crown Hill's public art displays.

Sarah Tittle Barrett Bolton was considered Indiana's unofficial "poet-laureate" during the 1840s and 50s. She penned the poem "Paddle Your Own Canoe," which was set to music and performed worldwide. During the Civil War, Bolton wrote "Union Forever," a poem that rallied the North to continue the fight.

Poet James Whitcomb Riley wrote more than 1,000 poems with humor and sentimentality, mainly children's poems and midwestern poems in dialect. He was known as the "National Poet," the "People's Poet Laureate," the "Hoosier Poet," and the "Children's Poet."

Author and playwright Newton Booth Tarkington wrote several successful books about life in the Midwest. He also wrote several plays about changing cultural values and the middle class. During his fifty-year career, Tarkington was awarded two Pulitzer Prizes.

Actor James Baskett performed on Broadway in 1929 with Louis Armstrong. His most famous role was in 1946 as Uncle Remus in Disney's *Song of the South*, where he sang the song, "Zip-a-dee-do-dah." Baskett received an honorary Academy Award for his performance.

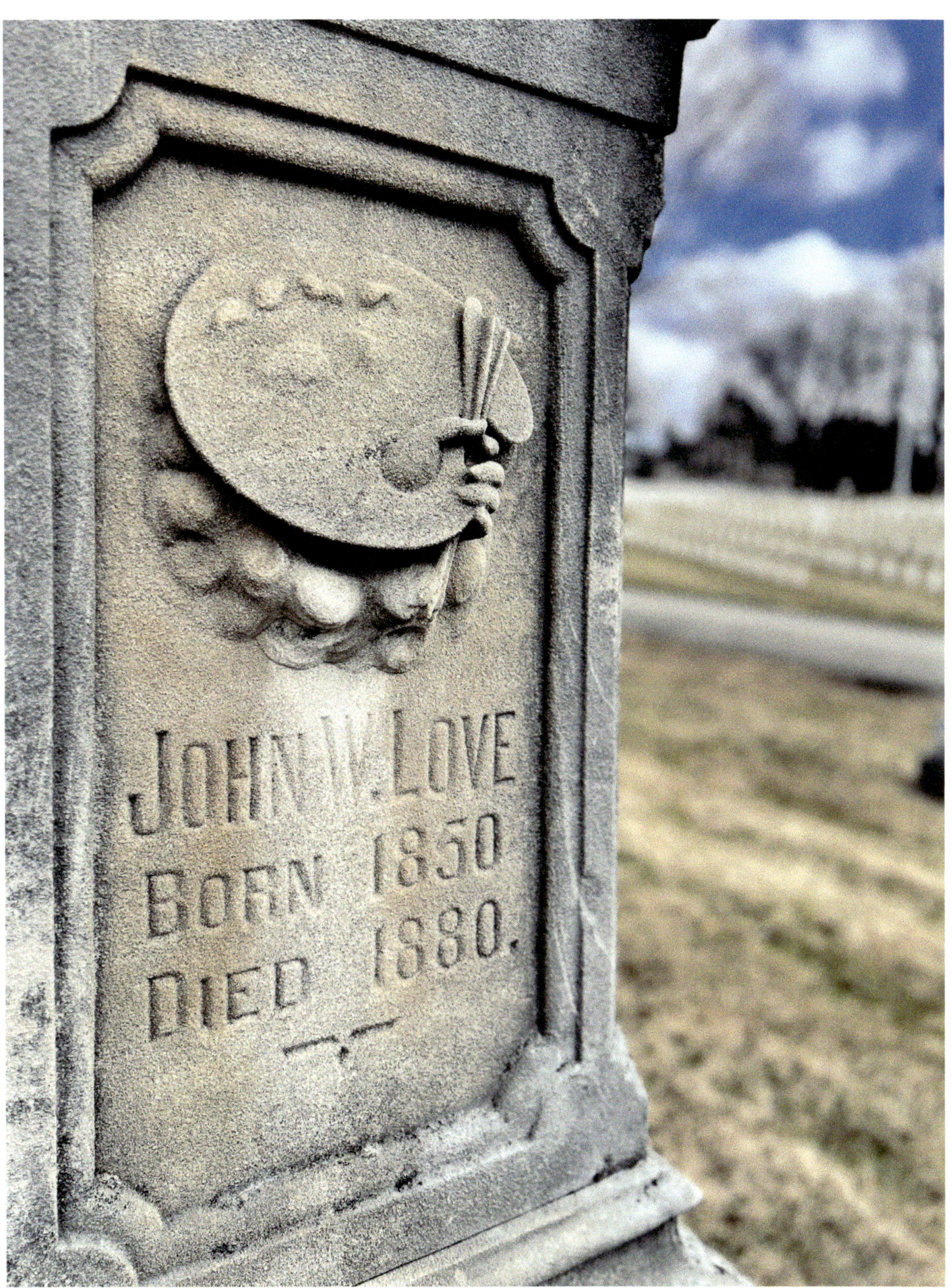

John Washington Love (August 10, 1850 – June 24, 1880) was a renowned Hoosier artist. His career as a painter ended when he died at the age of thirty. An eye-catching bas-relief stone shows an artist's hand holding a paint palette and brushes. (Section 3, Lot 3) *[Marcus Collins]*

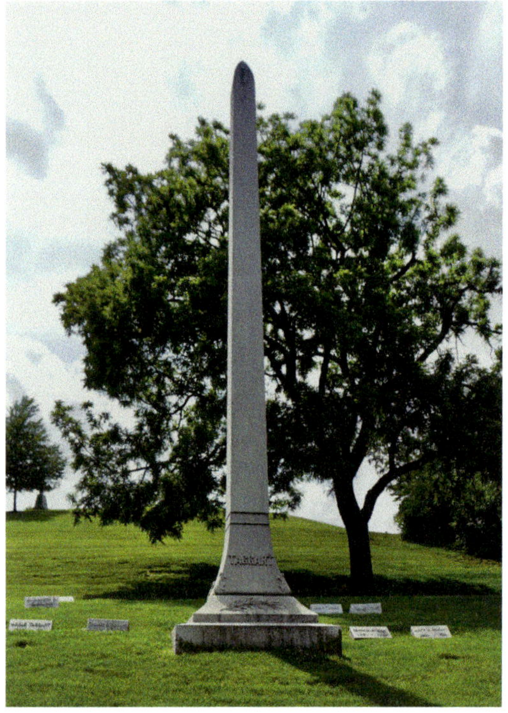

Lucy Martha Taggart (March 7, 1880 – October 9, 1960) was a portrait painter trained at the Herron School of Art in Indianapolis, where she later taught. A soaring obelisk with a palm frond at the base, signifying triumph over death, marks the Taggart family graves. (Section 30, Lot 3)

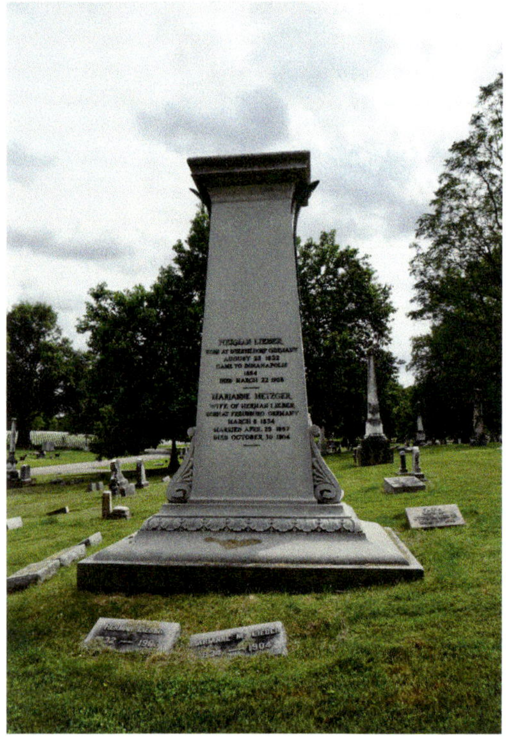

Herman Lieber (August 23, 1832 – March 22, 1908) was an Indianapolis patron of the arts. On the sides of his tall monument are decorative scrolls depicting the story of life and tall ferns for humility, which reach the top. (Section 5, Lot 70)

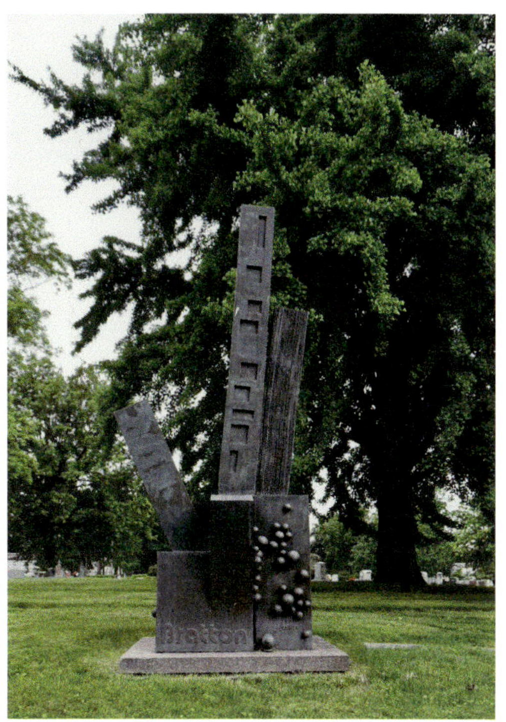

Right: Jeffrey Lawrence Bratton (February 12, 1957 – June 7, 1980) constructed his twelve-foot tall monument from bronze and granite. Seven columns burst out of the base at different angles while round spheres, or "bubbles," are placed randomly on the monument. (Section 75, Lot 1)

Below: Sarah Tittle Barrett Bolton (December 18, 1814 – August 5, 1893) was "Indiana's unofficial poet-laureate" during the mid-1800s. Her grave is marked with a simple marble headstone. (Section 5, Lot 14)

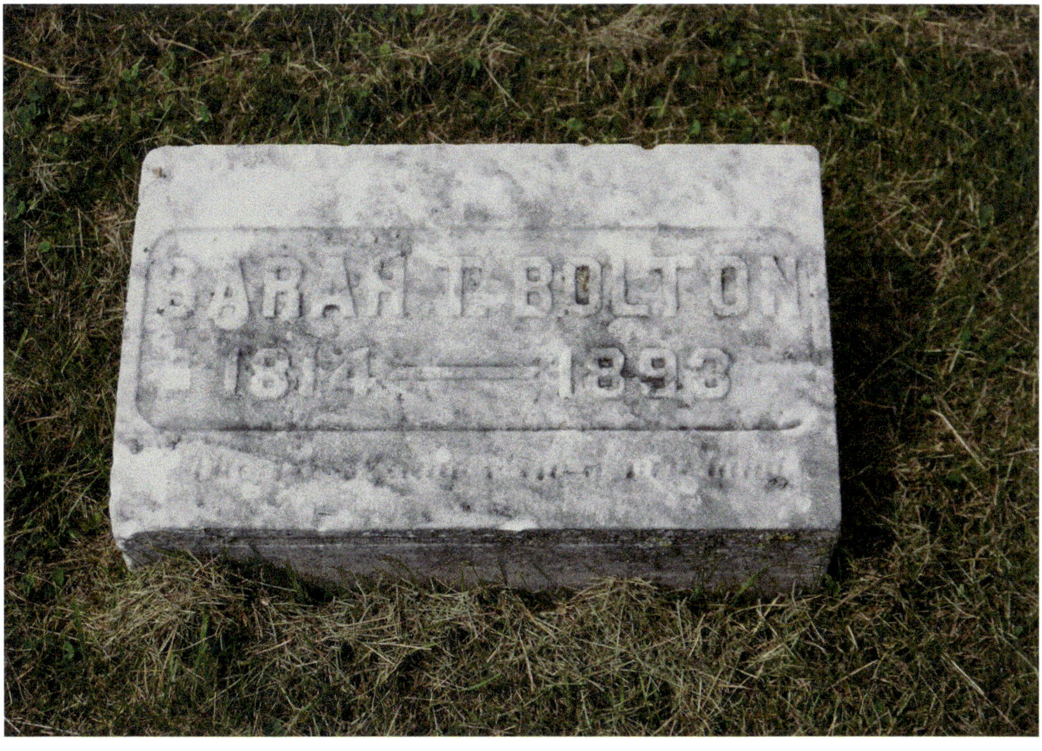

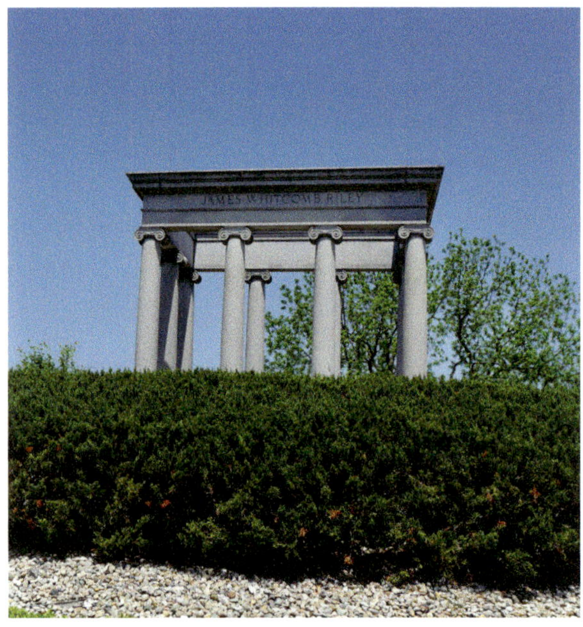

Poet James Whitcomb Riley (October 7, 1849 – July 22, 1916) wrote more than 1,000 poems. Known as the "National Poet" and the "People's Poet Laureate," ten pillars support the open-top frame of his stunning monument. (On the Crown)

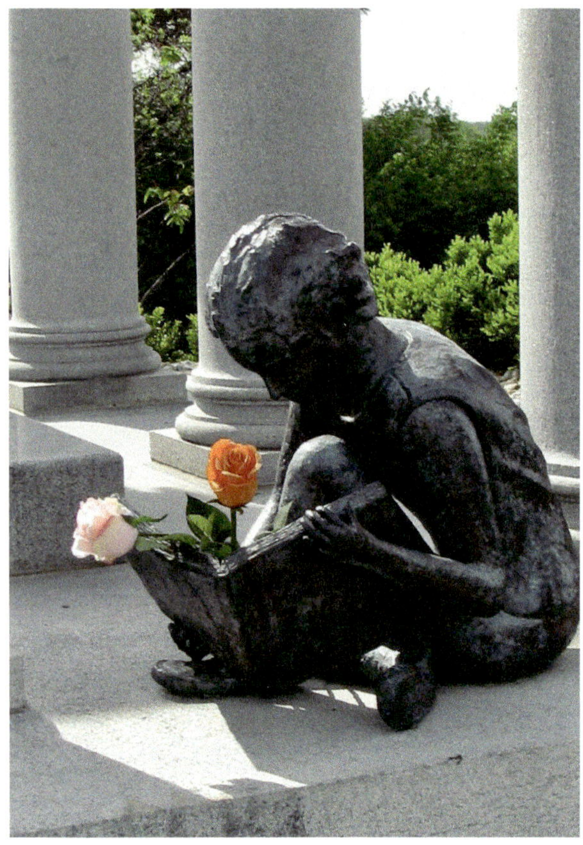

Inside the open-air Riley Memorial is a bronze statue of a child reading a book. Visitors leave flowers, coins, and gifts for her. (On the Crown)

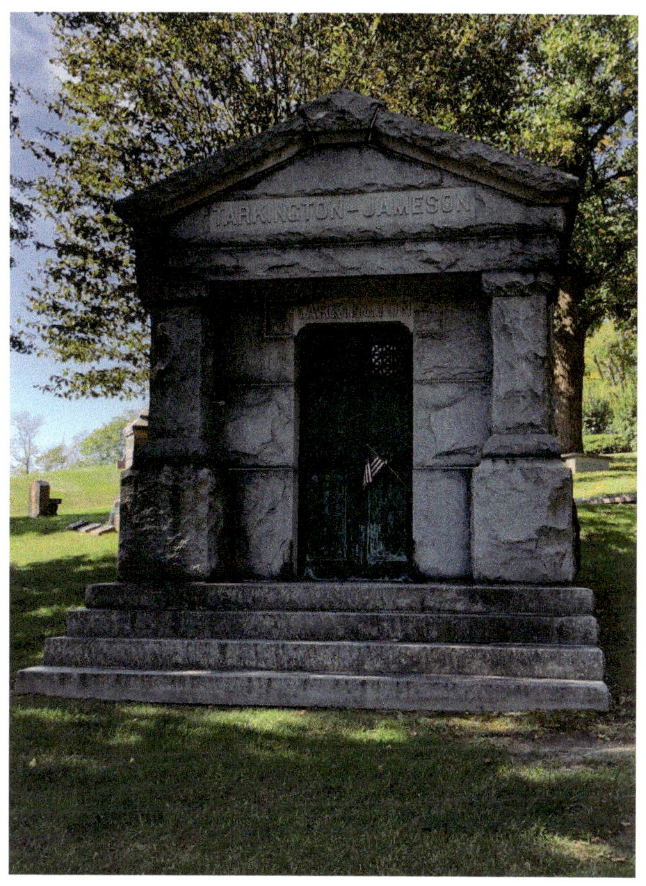

Right: Author and playwright Newton Booth Tarkington (July 29, 1869 – May 19, 1946) won two Pulitzer Prizes for his writing. His rough stone mausoleum sits atop a base with four steps leading to bronze double doors. (Section 56, Lot 13)

Below: Actor James Baskett (February 16, 1904 – July 9, 1948) received an honorary Academy Award for his performance in Disney's film, *Song of the South*. A grey granite stone mentions his character, Uncle Remus. (Section 37, Lot 602) *[Crown Hill Heritage Foundation]*

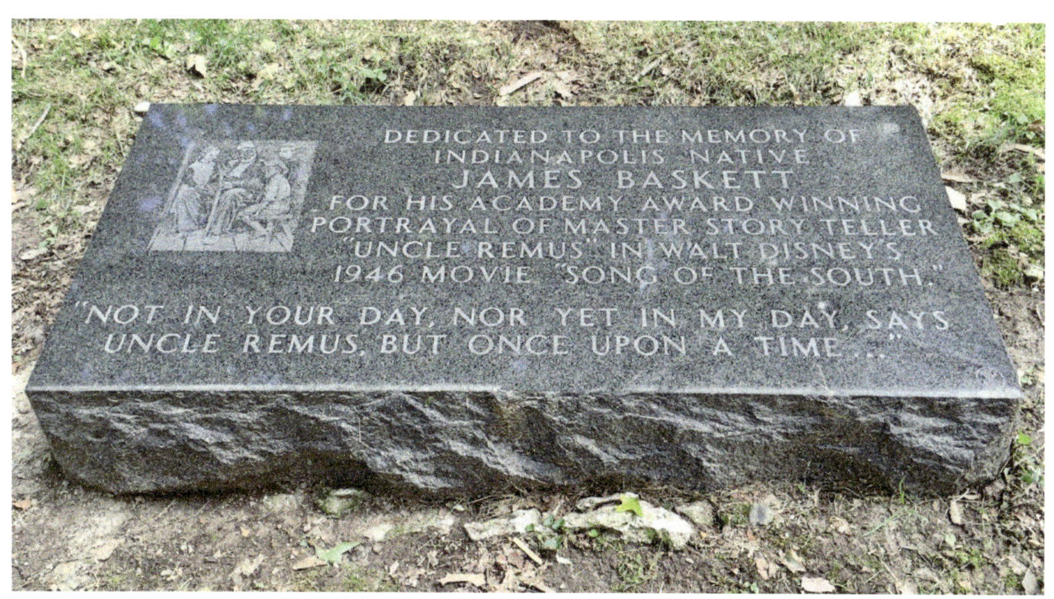

11
Heroes of Healthcare

From education and research to public health programs and rural health initiatives, Hoosiers have made substantial contributions to state and national healthcare. New procedures, along with specialized treatments and innovative medical devices, have been developed here.

Recognition goes to those like Dr. John Stough Bobbs, who performed the first gallbladder surgery in Indianapolis in 1867 and went on to establish the Indiana Medical College in 1869. William Brooks Fortune, Ph.D., developed numerous medical products, including antibiotics, blood sugar testing devices, and refined the process of safely manufacturing the Salk polio vaccine. He also developed an aviation department for Eli Lilly to fly drugs worldwide.

African American doctors and medical workers were accepted in Indianapolis during the late nineteenth and early twentieth centuries. The first licensed African American physician in the state was Dr. Samuel A. Elbert, who was appointed to the Indianapolis Board of Health, where he served as president. Dr. Sumner Alexander Furniss broke several racial barriers, becoming the first African American to serve with local, state, and national medical organizations. Dr. Furniss founded Lincoln Hospital, the first African American hospital in Indiana, while Dr. Joseph Henry Ward founded the city's first surgical hospital for African Americans. Dr. George Hosea Rawls was one of the first African American surgeons in Indianapolis. He also served as president of the Marion County Medical Society, the Indiana State Medical Society, and the Aesculapian Medical Society. Rawls received two Sagamore of the Wabash awards and authored five medical books.

The medical field was slower to accept women into its ranks. Dr. Helene Elise Hermine Knabe was a pioneering bacteriologist who proved the existence of rabies. She was the first woman to hold a departmental chair at Indiana Veterinary College and served as superintendent at the State Board of Health. But in 1911, Knabe was murdered. Her case was mishandled, and no one was convicted. It remains a cold case.

Pharmaceuticals were also a growing field in Indiana. Colonel Eli Lilly was a pharmacist and chemist who founded Eli Lilly and Company in 1876. His company revolutionized the pharmaceutical industry. John August Hook opened the first Hook's Drug Store in 1900 and quickly expanded to twelve stores. By the 1920s, Hook's Drug

Stores were in more than forty neighborhoods in the Indianapolis area. Son August F. "Bub" Hook began expanding the chain throughout Indiana. By 1972, Hook's had more than 150 self-serve stores, with more than 400 by 1994.

Crown Hill Cemetery features several monuments that honor those individuals who have contributed to medical research. The Indiana AIDS Memorial honors those who lost their lives to AIDS (acquired immunodeficiency syndrome), as well as caregivers and advocates. This was the first permanent AIDS Memorial in any cemetery, the first in the Midwest, and one of only four AIDS Memorials in the country in 2000. The Medical Science Donor Memorial honors individuals who have donated their bodies to science for the advancement of medical education and research. The Heroes of Public Safety Memorial is dedicated to honoring law enforcement officers, firefighters, and emergency technicians who have died in the line of duty. Nearly 1,000 public safety officers are currently remembered here.

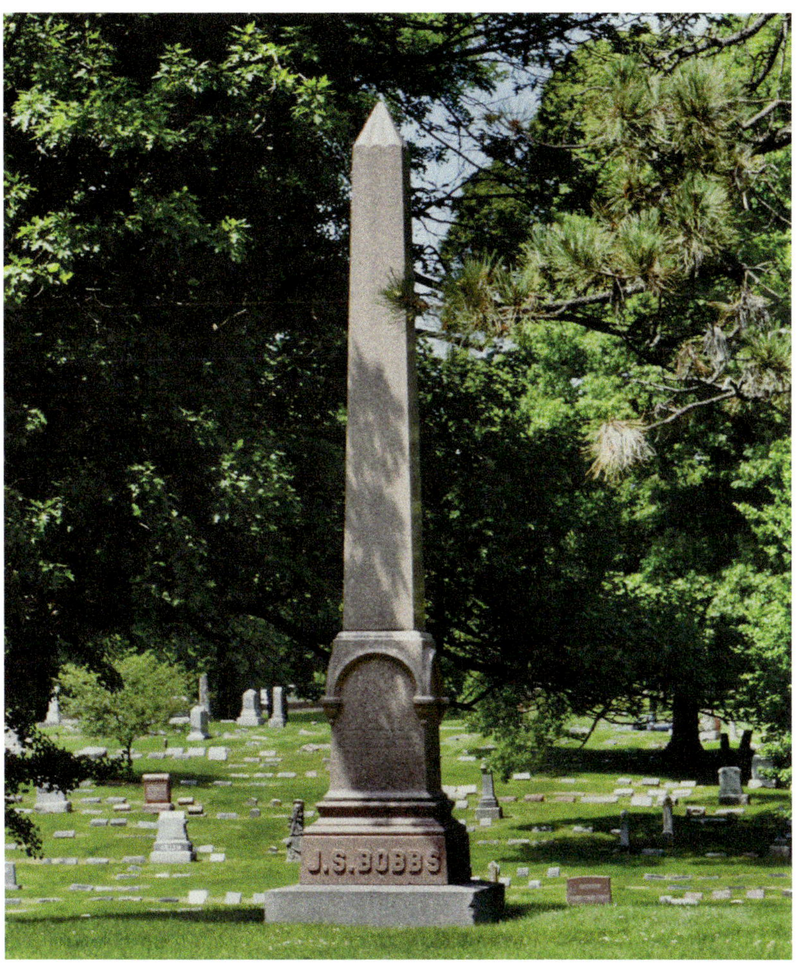

Dr. John Stough Bobbs (December 22, 1809 – May 1, 1870) performed the first successful gallbladder surgery in the country. He also served two terms as an Indiana senator. His obelisk is made of red granite. (Section 7, Lot 53)

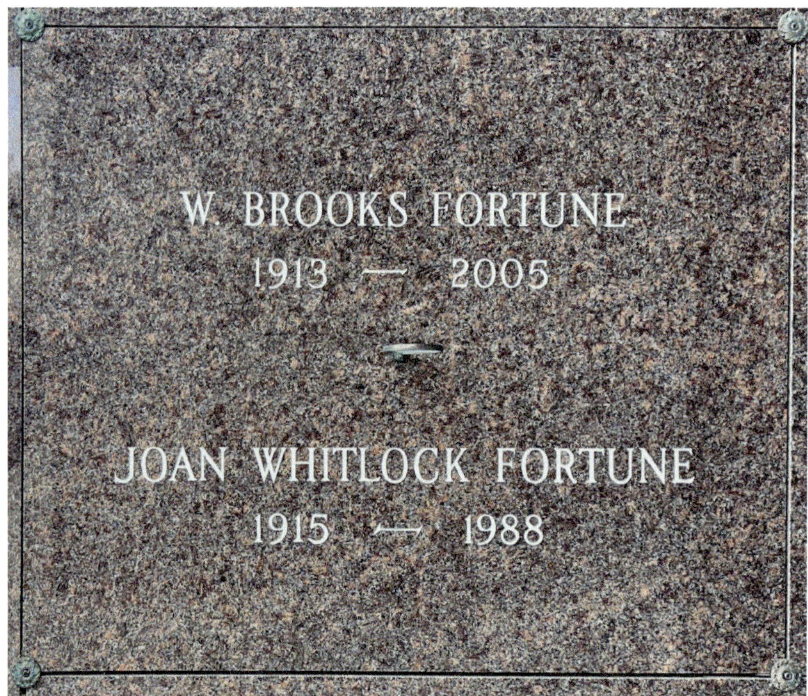

William Brooks Fortune, Ph.D. (July 2, 1913 – February 16, 2005) was a prominent Indianapolis scientist and philanthropist. The Fortune family mausoleum crypt is sealed with red granite. (Garden Mausoleum V, Crypt E-11)

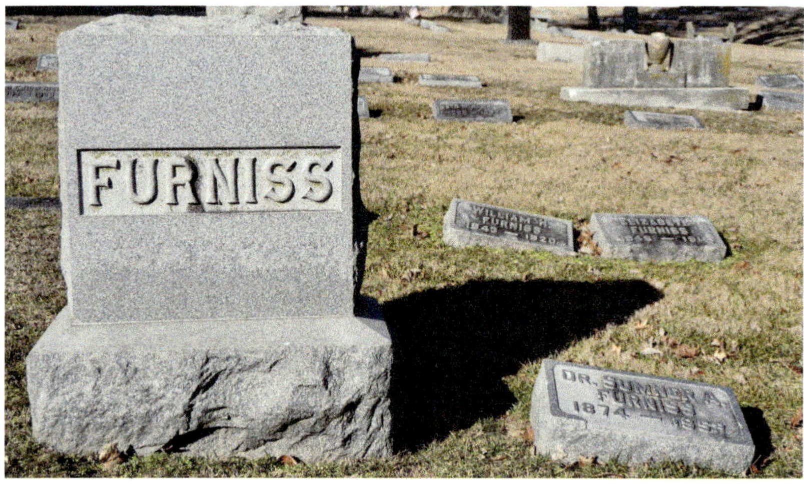

Dr. Sumner Alexander Furniss (January 30, 1874 – January 18, 1953) was among the few African American doctors to gain membership in the Marion County (Indianapolis) Medical Society, Indiana State Medical Society, and American Medical Association. Rounded, raised lettering adorns his family marker as family headstones rest nearby. (Section 47, Lot 64)

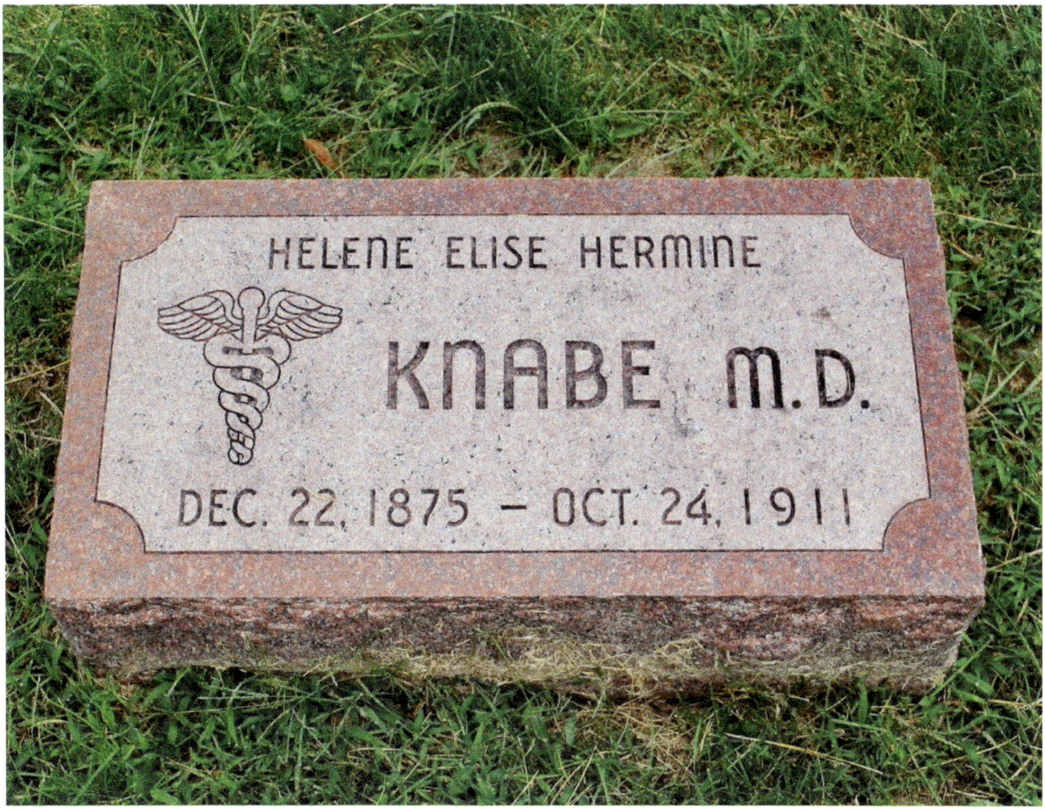

Above: Dr. Helene Elise Hermine Knabe (December 22, 1875 – October 24, 1911) was a physician, medical illustrator, and suffragist. She proved the existence of rabies in Indiana and dedicated herself to finding a treatment. Dr. Knabe was murdered in 1911. Her killer was never caught. (Section 43, Lot 6950) *[Find a Grave]*

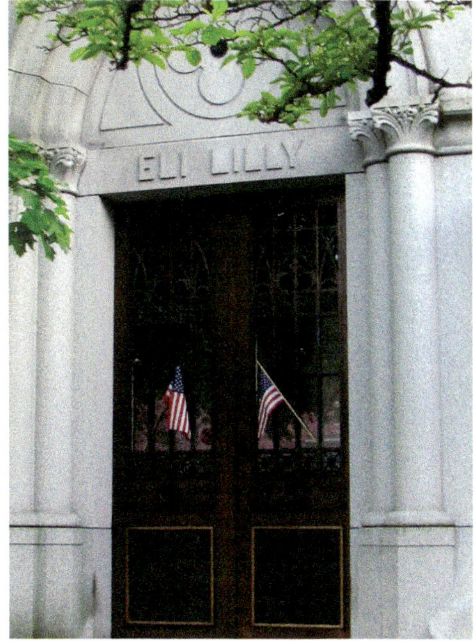

Right: Colonel Eli Lilly (July 8, 1838 – June 6, 1898) founded Eli Lilly and Company in 1876, which became the largest corporation in Indiana. Lilly's reforms for the pharmaceutical industry resulted in the creation of the Food and Drug Administration (FDA). His neo-classical mausoleum is the final resting place for several family members. (Section 13, Lot 19)

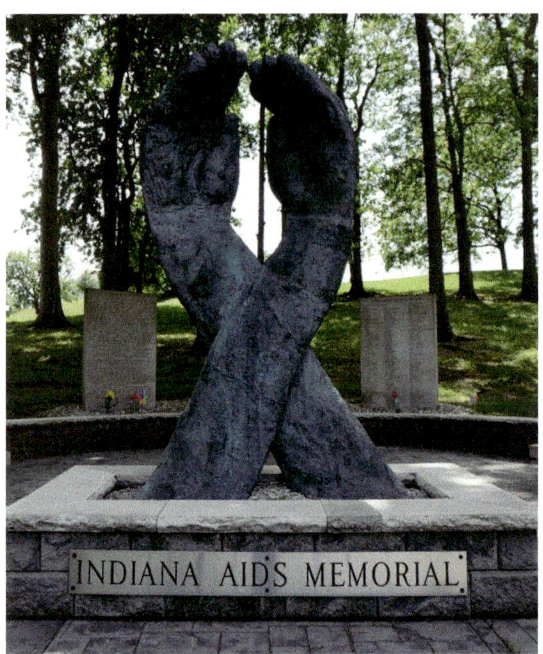

Left: The Indiana AIDS Memorial was the first permanent AIDS (Acquired Immunodeficiency Syndrome) memorial located in a cemetery in the United States, and one of only four placed in the country in 2000. Indianapolis sculptor Guy R. Grey crafted two 10-foot crossed bronze arms with cupped hands that form the shape of the AIDS lapel ribbon. The markers in the background list the names of those who have died of AIDS. (Section 90, Northeast Corner)

Below: The Medical Science Donor Memorial, dedicated October 5, 2000, honors those who donated their bodies to medical science for continuing education. The monument is a rectangular granite wall with plaques marking the donors' final resting places. The brick path also contains burial urns. (Section 41, Lot 298)

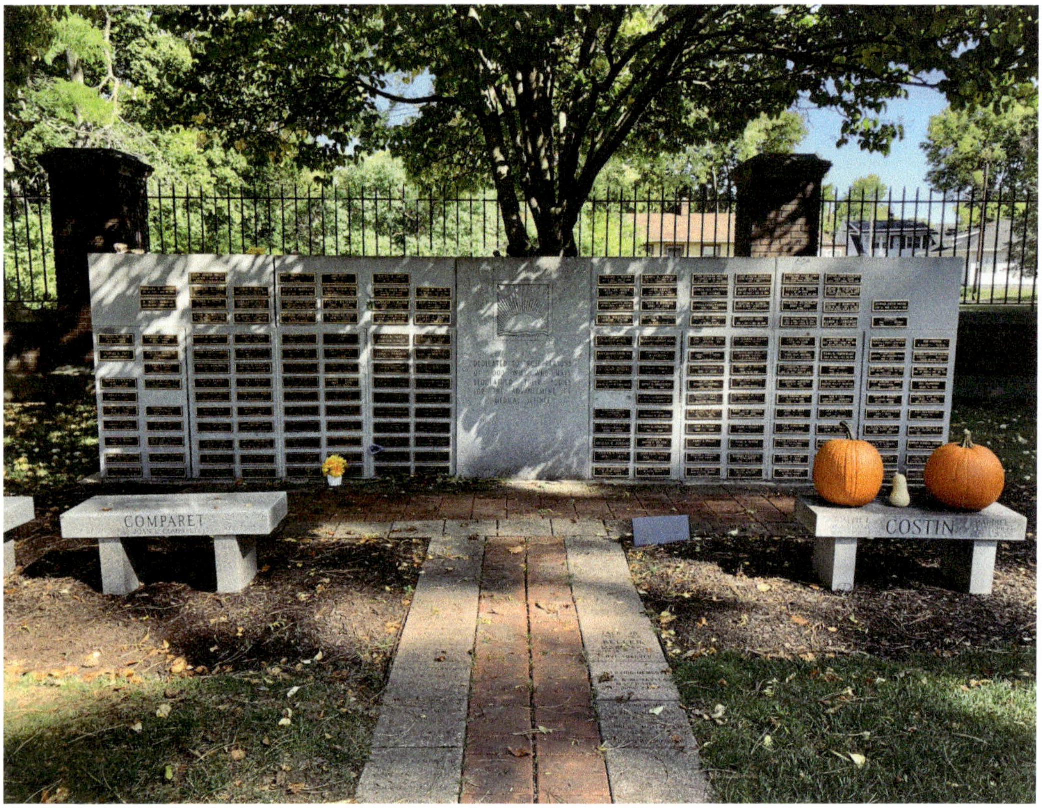

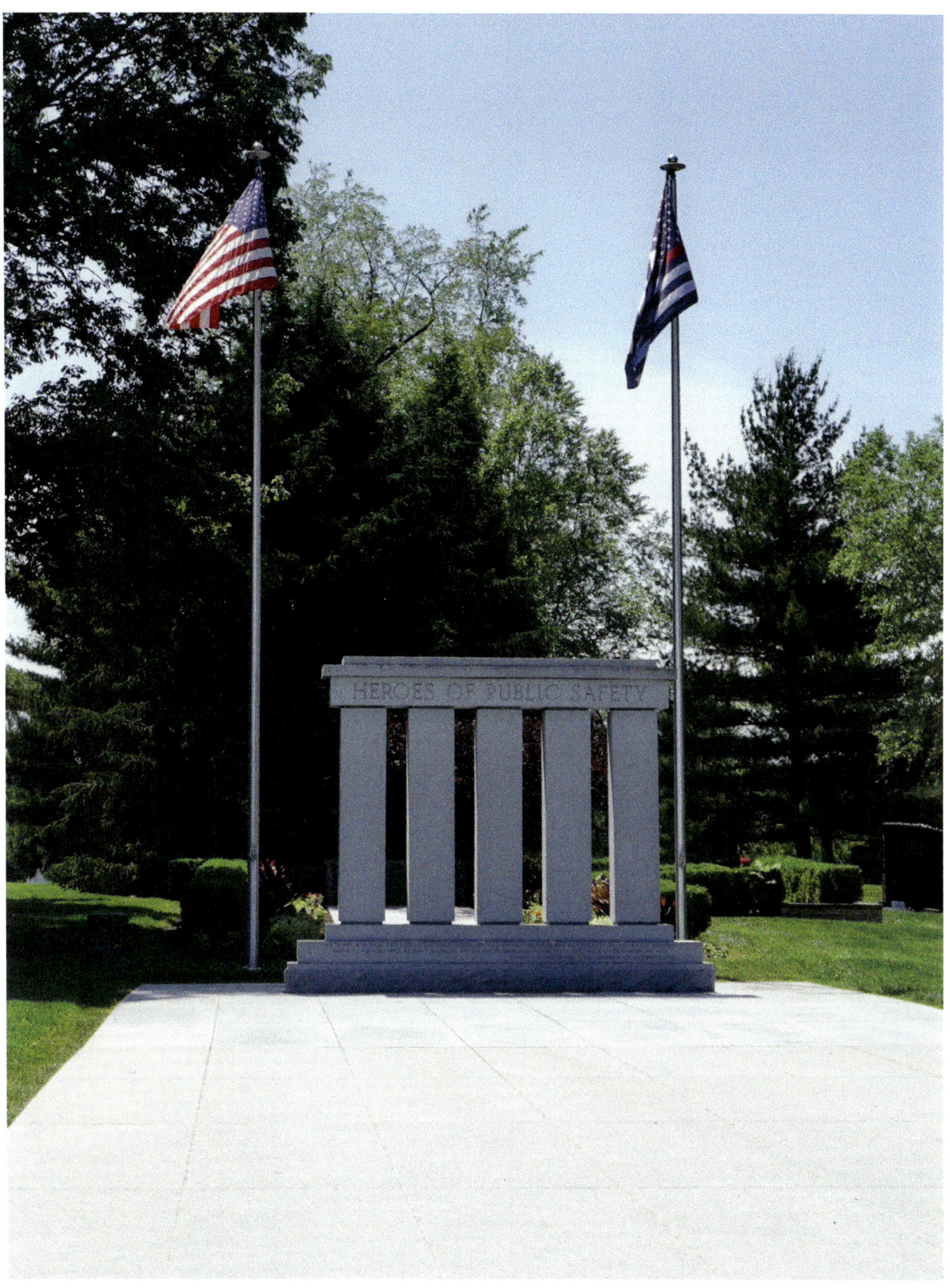

The Heroes of Public Safety Memorial, dedicated September 14, 2002, honors those who made the ultimate sacrifice in public service. There are nearly 1,000 public safety personnel remembered here. (Section 97, Lot 4010)

12
Motor City Legends of Racing

More than sixty racing legends are interred at Crown Hill, along with others who played a part in automotive history. The four founding fathers of racing, Carl Fisher, James Allison, Frank Wheeler, and Arthur Newby, lie among Indy 500 winners, drivers, mechanics, racing media, and others involved in the sport. Founded by the Indiana Motor Speedway (IMS), the track was built in Speedway, Indiana, using three-million bricks. In 1911, the first 500-mile race was held on Memorial Day. The Indy 500 has been held every Memorial Day since, except during World War I and World War II.

The Final Finish Line was laid as a tribute to the founders and racecar drivers of the IMS and marks the completion of life's race. The Final Finish Line was created from original Brickyard culver bricks and runs in front of founder Carl Fisher's mausoleum.

The Four Founders of the Indianapolis Motor Speedway and The Indy 500

Carl Graham Fisher was the "father" of the Indy 500. Working with friends, Fisher co-founded Prest-O-Lite Battery Company with his long-time friend, James Asbury Allison. Fisher and Arthur Calvin Newby co-founded the Indianapolis Motor Speedway (IMS). And it was Fisher and co-founder Frank H. Wheeler who conceptualized holding a 500-mile race on a brick track. Wheeler had the IMS racetrack paved with three-million bricks for better driving performance and safety.

Racing Legends of the Indy 500

Numerous racecar drivers have contributed to the sport. One was engineer Louis Schwitzer, who won the first auto race held at the Indianapolis Motor Speedway in 1909. Driver Howard Samuel "Howdy" Wilcox was the only racer to drive in the first eleven Indy 500 races. Wilcox won the 1919 Indy 500 and was the first driver to qualify at 100 miles-per-hour.

Driver Charles C. Merz raced during the early years and later became the Chief Steward of the Memorial Day Classic. Racecar driver Louis Schneider was one of only two Indy 500 winners born in Indianapolis. Chester "Chet" Miller took part in sixteen Indy 500 races, driving more than 5,000 miles and earning the nickname, the "Dean of the Speedway." Miller was killed in a crash during practice for the 1953 Indy 500 race. James Ernest "Herk" Hurtubise won the 1960 Indianapolis 500 "Rookie of the Year" award. He drove in ten Indianapolis 500 races between 1960 and 1974. Paul Frank Russo raced in the Indy 500 fourteen times and finished in the Top Ten five times. And Erwin "Cannon Ball" Baker was a motorcycle and automobile racer known for endurance racing at the track. He became the first NASCAR Commissioner in 1947.

Indy 500 Support Staff

Charles H. Black was an innovator who imported a gasoline-powered German Benz engine and mounted it on a carriage in 1891. Black then drove the first "automobile" through the streets of Indianapolis, paving the way for a gasoline-powered car. Abraham Jacob "A.J." Watson was a mechanic and car builder who won Indy 500 acknowledgment numerous times.

Dr. Thomas Allen Hanna was the medical director at the Indianapolis 500 Speedway for several decades. He modernized the medical facilities at the raceway, improved emergency response, and endorsed better safety measures at racing events. Known as the "Voice of the Indianapolis 500" from 1990 to 1998, Robert "Bob" Jenkins provided play-by-play action of the Indy 500 races. Jenkins was inducted into the Indianapolis Motor Speedway Hall of Fame in 2019. Waldo Dane "Eddie" Edenburn became a well-known sportswriter for the *Indianapolis Star* and the *Detroit News*. He was the Chief Steward for the Indy 500 from 1919 to 1934.

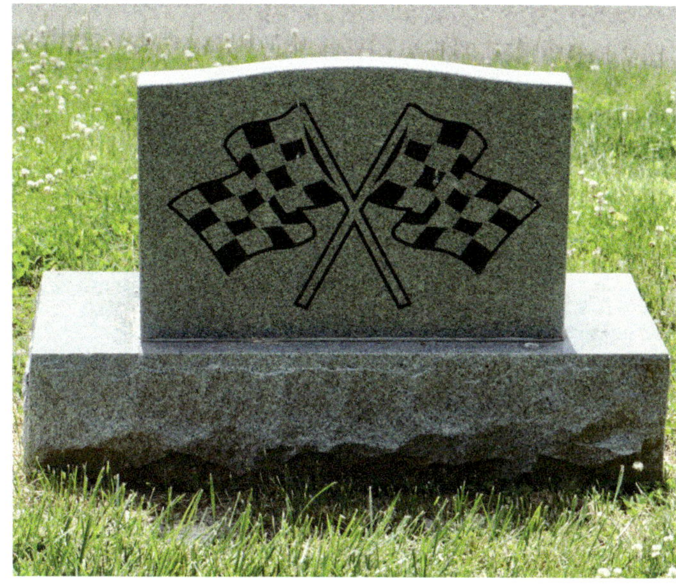

These checkered flags, engraved on the back of a gravestone, indicate the end of the race where someone is declared the winner. What a fitting marker for someone involved in the sport of racing. (Section 13)

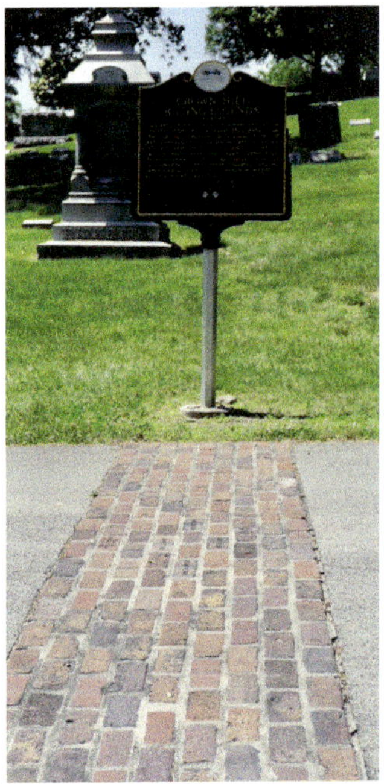

Left: The Final Finish Line was placed in the cemetery in 2017. This yard of bricks comes from the original Indiana Motor Speedway (IMS) Brickyard. The Final Finish Line runs in front of founder Carl Fisher's mausoleum. (Section 13)

Below: Carl Graham Fisher (January 12, 1874 – July 15, 1939) was the "father" of the Indy 500. Fisher helped develop the Lincoln Highway, the first east-west roadway in the U.S. He also assisted in developing Dixie Highway, running north-south from Michigan to Miami. His granite mausoleum was built in 1916 in the Egyptian style. (Section 13, Lot 42)

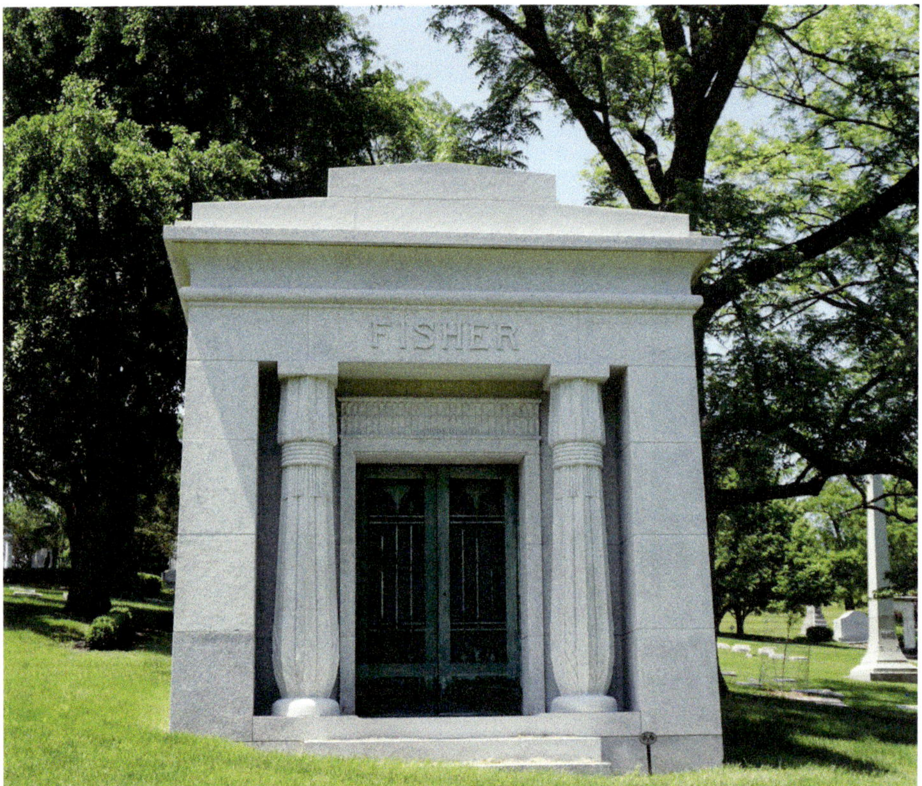

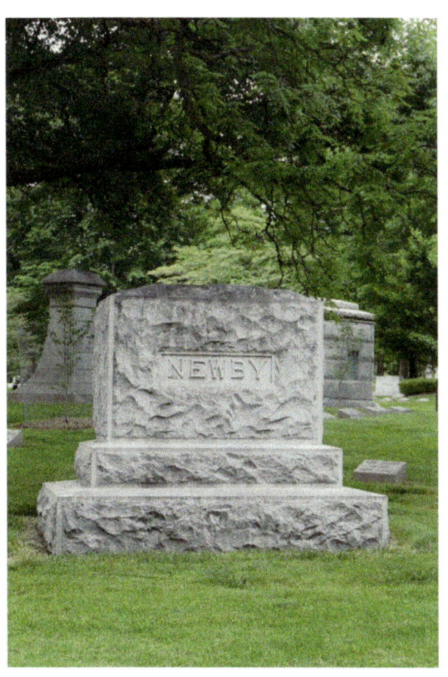

Right: Arthur Calvin Newby (December 29, 1865 – September 11, 1933) founded the National Motor Vehicle Company in 1900 and helped co-found the Indianapolis Motor Speedway in 1909. His gravestone is a roughly crafted monument set upon a base of two steps. (Section 23, Lot 39)

Below: The Crown Hill Racing plaque commemorates the four Speedway founders. James Asbury Allison (August 11, 1872 – August 4, 1928) was key to the success of the Indianapolis Motor Speedway and the Indianapolis 500. Allison became the sole owner of the Indianapolis Motor Speedway after the others died. Frank H. Wheeler (October 24, 1863 – May 27, 1921) and his financial contributions established the Indianapolis Motor Speedway. Wheeler also paved the raceway with bricks for safety.

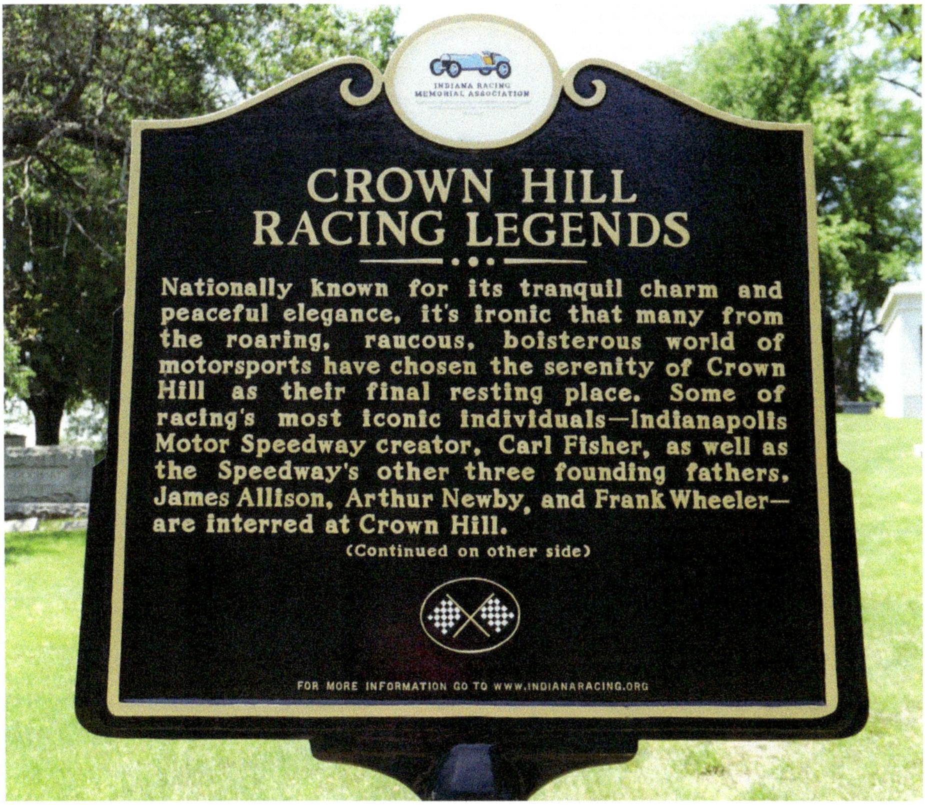

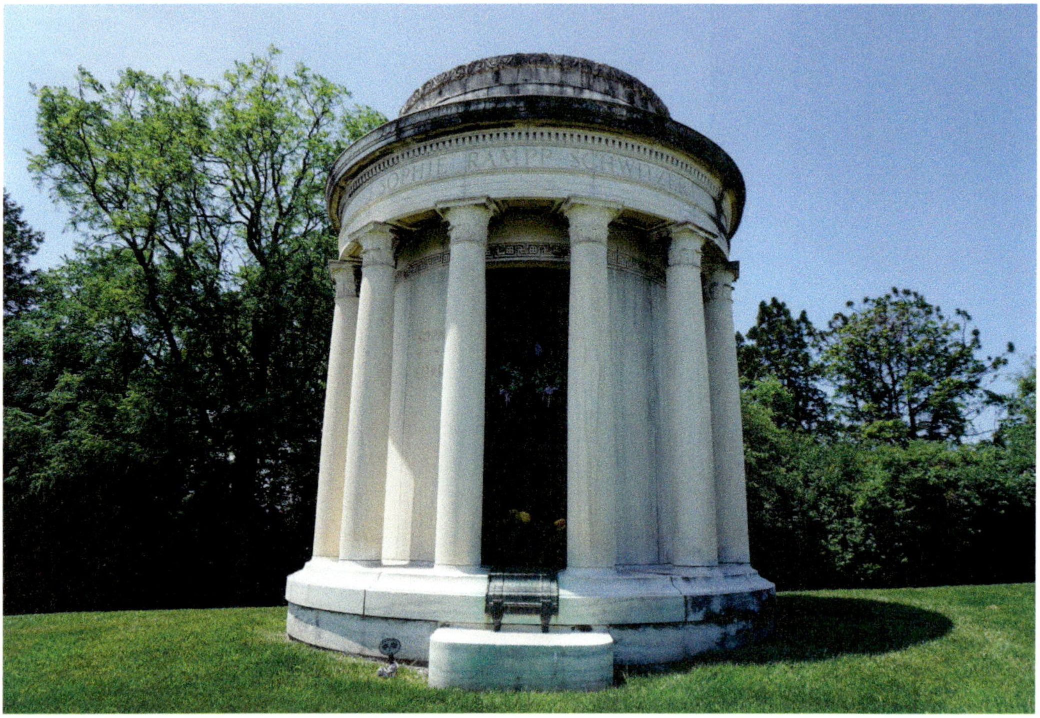

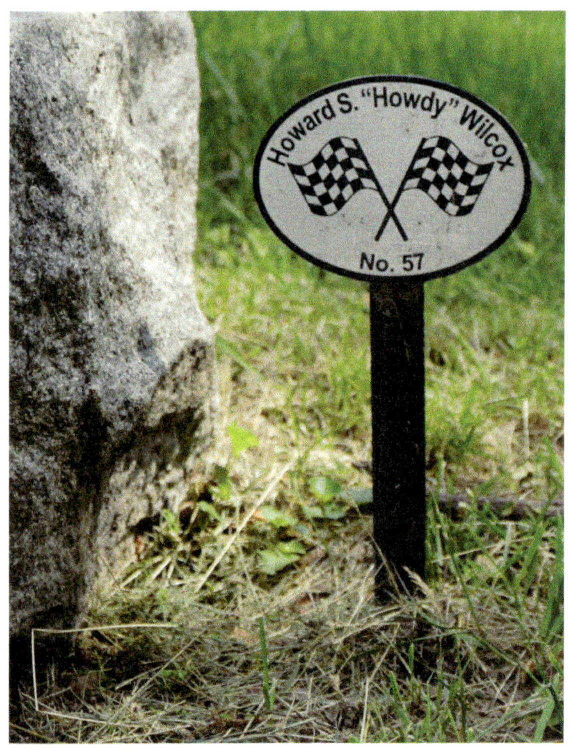

Above: Engineer Louis Schwitzer (February 29, 1880 – May 9, 1967) was honored in 1967, when the Society of Automotive Engineers (SAE) established the Louis Schwitzer Award, presented annually for design innovation at the 500. His mausoleum is a round neoclassical monument supported by several Doric columns. A bronze "carpet" leads to the double brass doors. (Section 61, Lot 3, On the Crown) *[Alessa Kivlehen]*

Left: Driver Howard Samuel "Howdy" Wilcox (June 24, 1889 – September 4, 1923) led the last 98 laps of the Indy 500 in 1919 to win the race. He was inducted into the Indianapolis Motor Speedway Hall of Fame posthumously in 1963. Next to his rough-cut stone, a checkered flag Racing Legends Plaque commemorates his participation in the Indy 500. (Section 56, Lot 240)

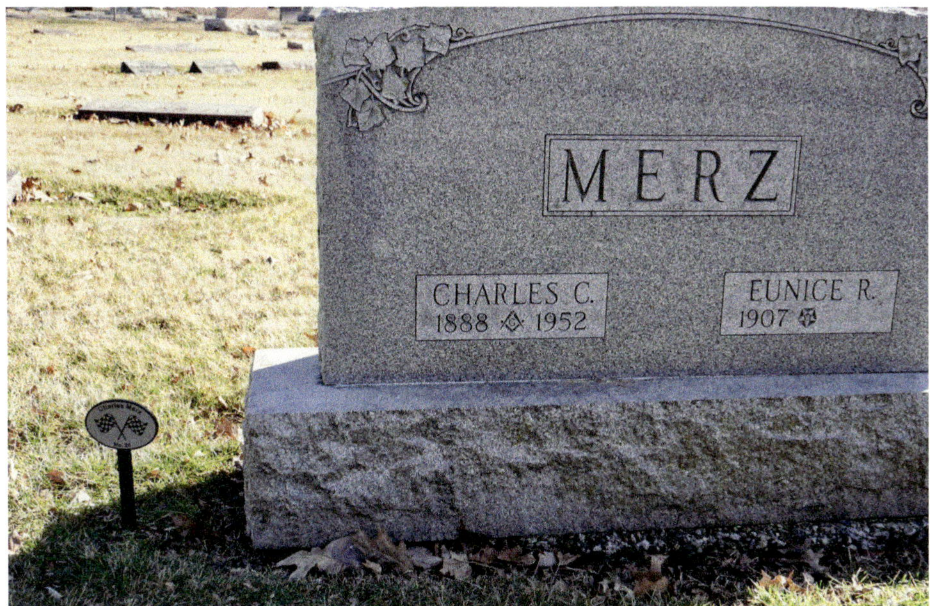

Driver Charles C. Merz's (July 6, 1888 – July 8, 1952) forte was distance racing. He set a driving distance record of 1,094 miles in 24 hours in 1905. Merz was Chief Steward for the Indy 500 Race from 1935 to 1939. (Section 62, Lot 223)

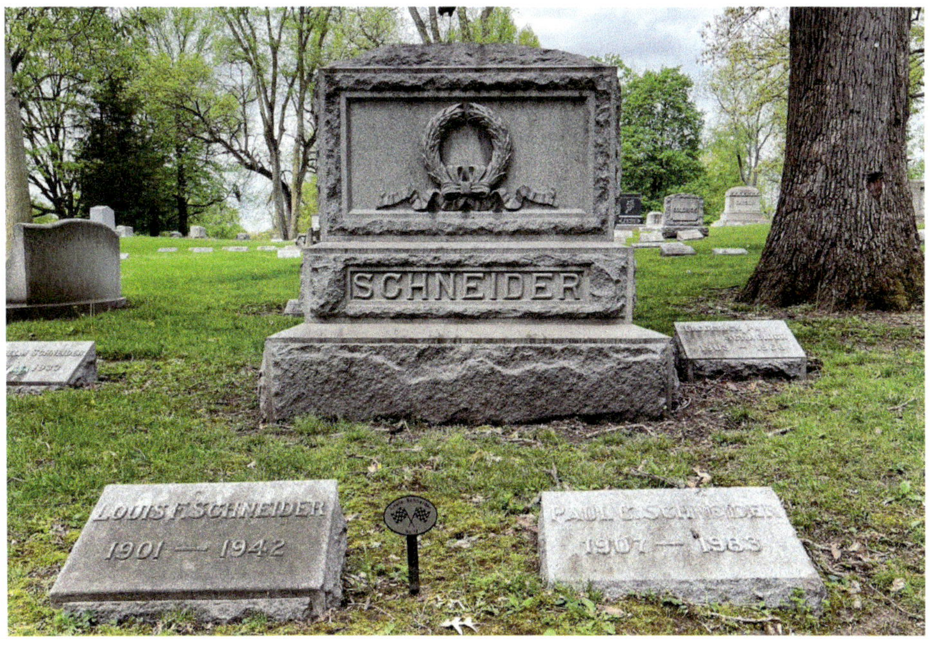

Driver Louise Schneider (December 19, 1901 – September 22, 1942) was one of only two local boys to race in the Indy 500. Schneider won the 1931 Indy 500. A laurel wreath of victory decorates the family monument. (Section 42, Lot 124) [*Crown Hill Heritage Foundation*]

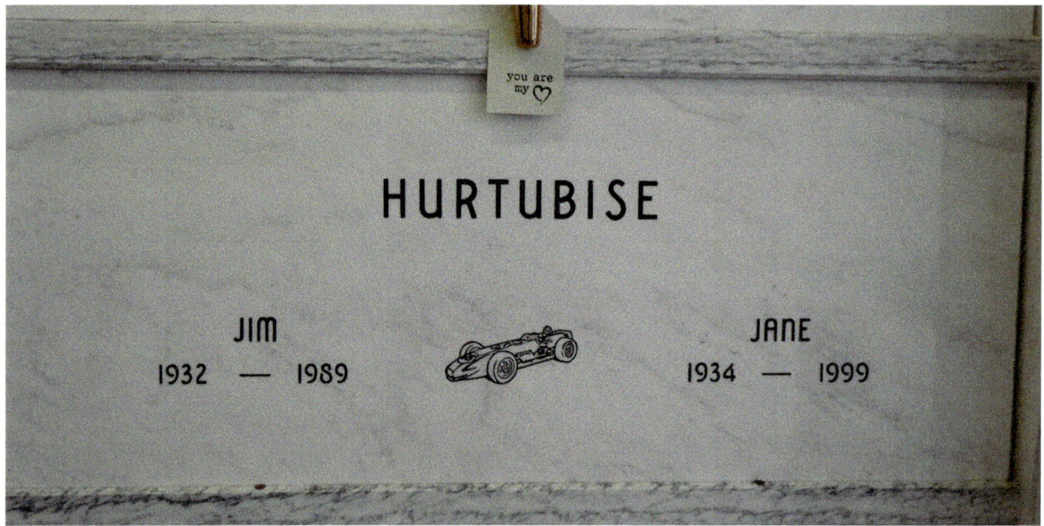

Racecar driver James Ernest "Herk" Hurtubise (December 5, 1932 – January 6, 1989) was named Indianapolis 500 "Rookie of the Year" in 1960, coming within three miles-per-hour (mph) of breaking the 150-mph speed mark. A racecar bearing the number 56 is etched on his mausoleum crypt. (Community Mausoleum, Corridor D, Row 8, Level 2, Depth D)

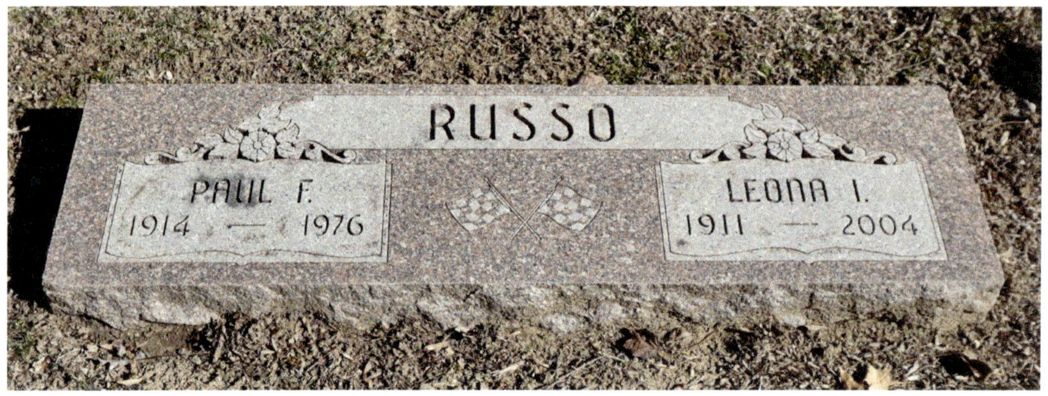

Driver Paul Frank Russo (April 10, 1914 – February 13, 1976) competed in the American Automobile Association (AAA) Eastern Midget Champion and the United States Auto Club (USAC) Championship Car series, driving in eighty-one races over twenty-two years. Two crossed checker flags, signaling the end of the race, are etched on his red granite stone. (Section 78, Lot 83)

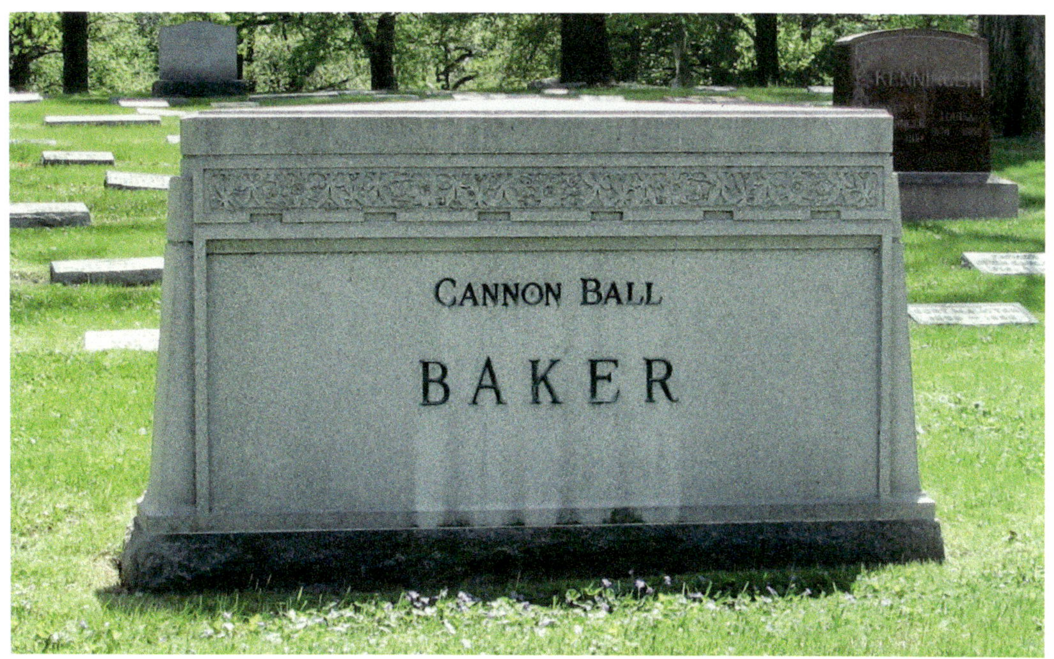

Above: Erwin "Cannon Ball" Baker (March 12, 1882 – May 10, 1960) was known for motorcycle racing on the Indy track, which earned him the nickname "Cannon Ball." Baker was inducted into the Indianapolis Motor Speedway Hall of Fame, Motorsports Hall of Fame of America, and American Motorcyclist Association Motorcycle Hall of Fame. (Section 60, Lot 150)

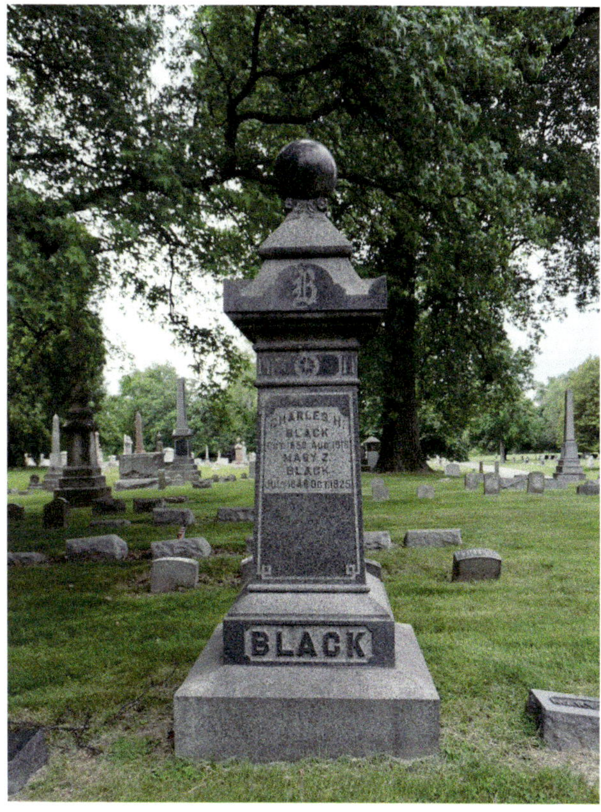

Right: Charles H. Black (October 5, 1850 – August 19, 1918) made numerous innovations in the automobile field, including building a gasoline-powered carriage with a Karl Benz engine. His grave is marked with a black granite monument topped with a solid granite ball. (Section 25, Lot 185)

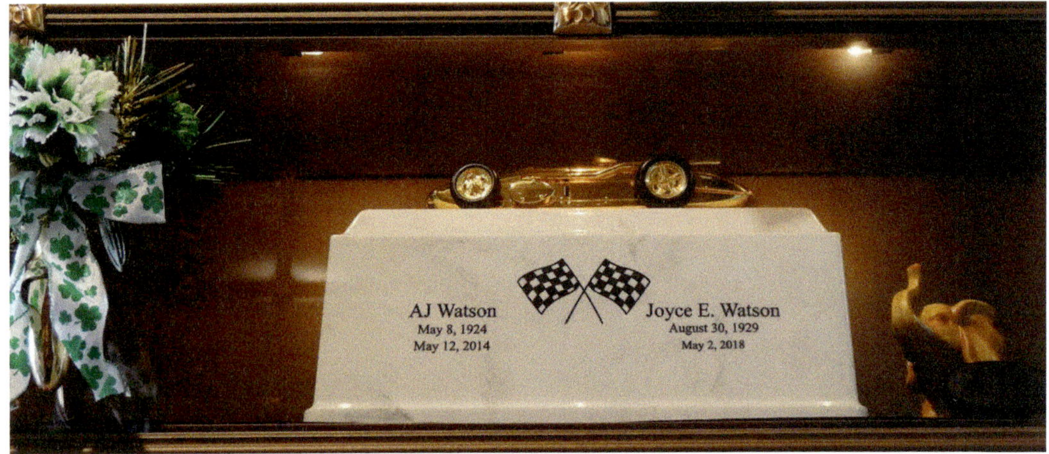

Car builder Abraham Jacob "A. J." Watson (May 8, 1924 – May 12, 2014) built six cars that won the Indianapolis 500. A gold racecar sits atop his marble cremains box, which bears the crossed checker flags. (Community Mausoleum, Niche F 153)

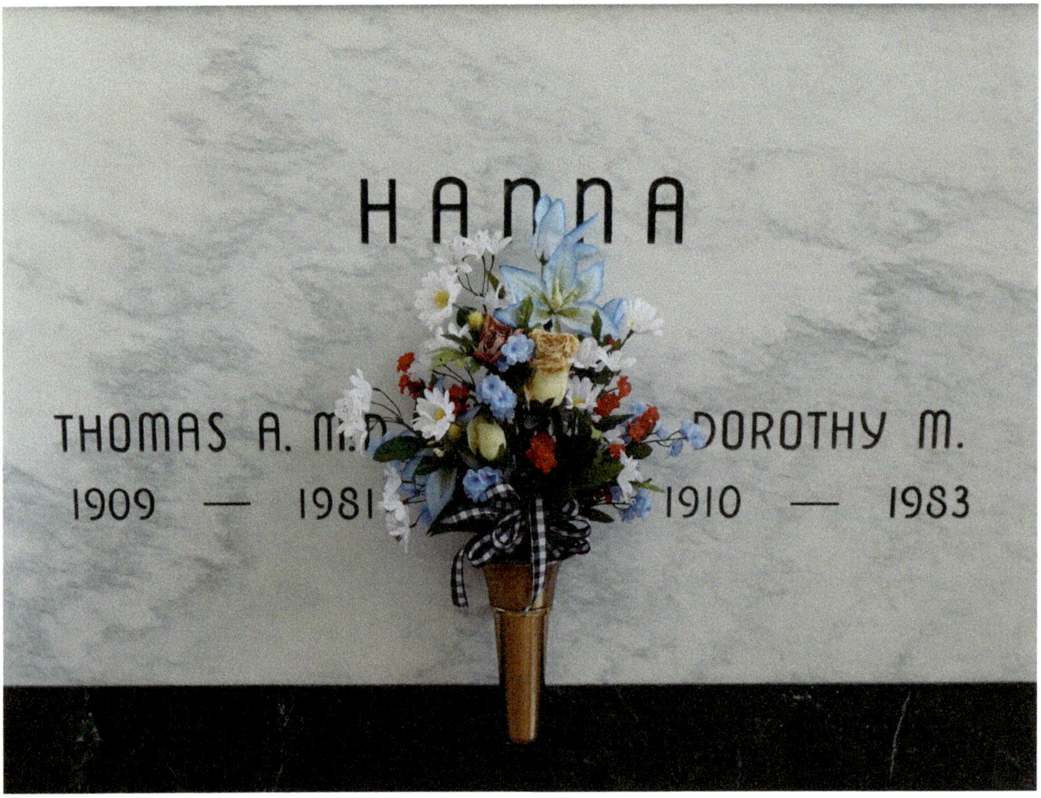

Dr. Thomas Allen Hanna (September 4, 1909 – November 12, 1981) served as the Indianapolis Motor Speedway's medical doctor and director for decades. His crypt is sealed with white marble. (Community Mausoleum, Corridor F, Row 14, Level E)

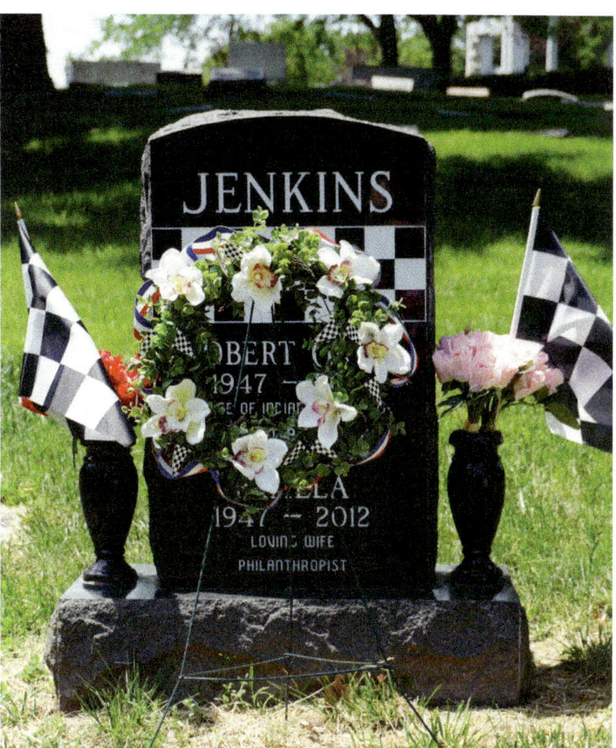

Right: Robert "Bob" Jenkins (September 4, 1947 – August 9, 2021) was the "Voice of the Indianapolis 500." His stone bears the winning checkered flag pattern along with a quote, "I'm just a race fan that got lucky." (Section 13, Lot 45)

Below: Waldo Dane "Eddie" Edenburn (September 27, 1885 – September 21, 1934) served as the Chief Steward for the Indy 500 from 1919 to 1934. A red granite headstone marks his grave. (Section 60, Lot 713)

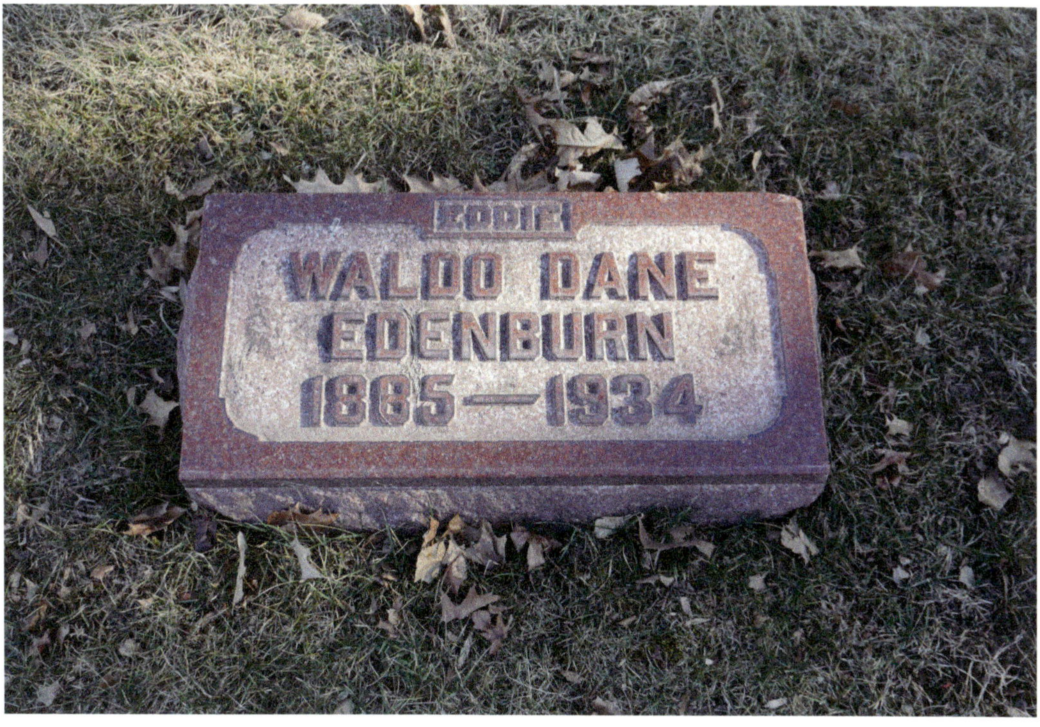

13
Crown Hill's Amazing Monuments and Stories

There is something awe-inspiring about historic monuments and markers, especially in a cemetery. Not only do these memorials help people better understand and remember significant events, but they also showcase works of artistic and cultural expression that encourage deeper contemplation.

The monument to Albertina Allen Forrest is the most dramatic funerary art in Crown Hill. It depicts a grief-stricken woman weeping for all that could have been. (Forrest died suddenly of a cerebral hemorrhage just before her thirty-second birthday.) The monument is recorded by the Smithsonian Institute as "Woman in Repose, sculpted by Rudolf Schwarz (1866 – 1912) in bronze on a granite base."

Many of the cemetery's mausoleums are intriguing and awe-inspiring. Hotelier George Joseph Marott was known for his magnificent Marott Hotel, which featured two ten-story towers with a Spanish-style garden, dining room, and ballrooms on the first floor. The Fortiter Castle Mausoleum is a recent addition to the cemetery, and is protected by a bronze lion at the entrance of the "drawbridge." The Brammer Mausoleum is constructed of granite in an octagonal shape with detailed floral artwork at the windows. Both were built in 2023 by Gibraltar Mausoleum Services, owned by Jay Brammer.

The statues of two children touch the hearts of many visitors. Mary Ella McGinnis was five-years-old when she died of lung congestion. An Italian sculptor carved a life-like marble statue of the child, and visitors leave flowers and toys in Mary Ella's arms as a tribute to her short life. Corliss Randle Ruckle died at the age of eleven from the "strangling angel," diphtheria. His life-sized marble statue reminds visitors that life can be fleeting.

Three Indianapolis women moved to a different beat during their lifetimes. Avriel Joy Shull enrolled in the John Herron Art Institute but never graduated. She founded Avriel Art Associates in 1948, and six years later built a mid-century modern home as a self-trained architect. Shull designed the Carmel, Indiana, neighborhood, "Thornhurst," in her modern style. It's listed on the National Register of Historic Places.

Elfrieda Mais Hellman LaPlante was a daredevil airplane wing-walker and stunt driver. Seeking bigger thrills, she began racing cars under the name of "Mais" in 1912, but being a woman, she was not allowed to race on any track. LaPlante was killed after driving through a wall of fire at the Alabama State Fair.

Helen Essie Kegerreis Link was known for her love of daffodils. Her home had seventeen acres with more than 1,100 varieties. Her daffodils are maintained by the Indiana Daffodil Society.

Crown Hill also has two twin angels. One is a bronze statue on the pink granite Eli Lilly monument. The other is on the stained-glass window in the Peace Chapel in the Community Mausoleum. Both are known as the Lilly Family Peace Angels.

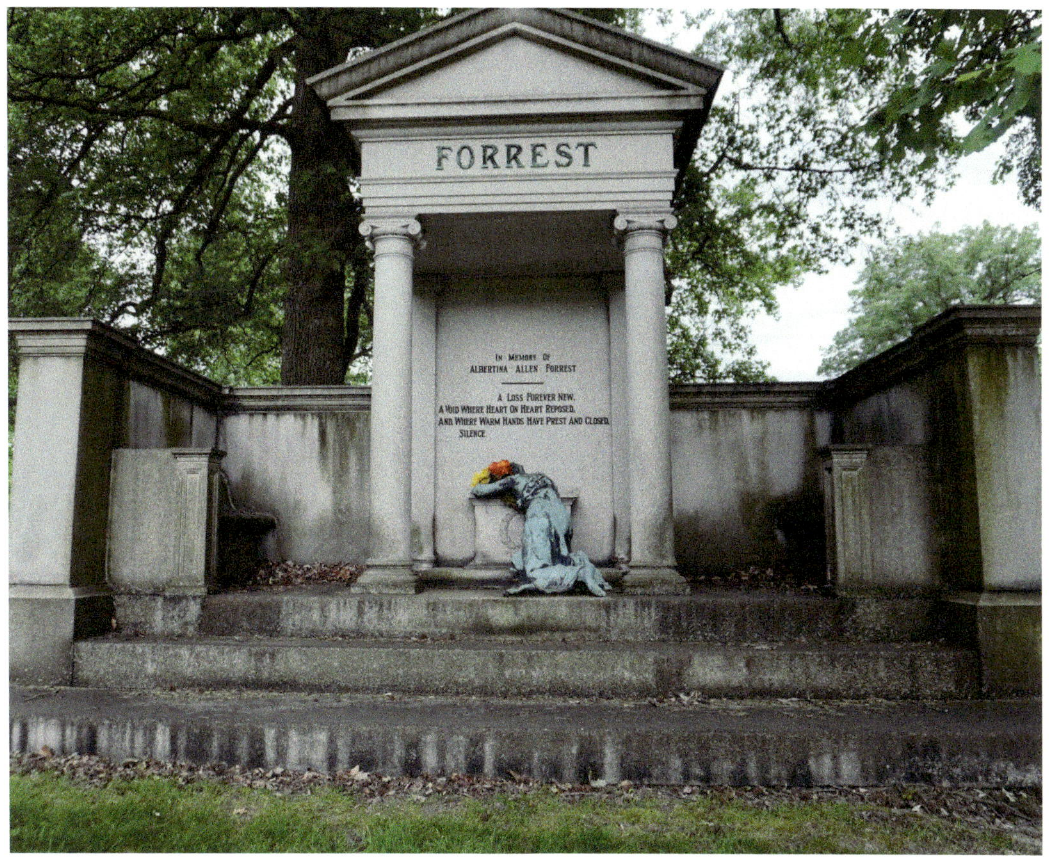

The monument for Albertina Allen Forrest (May 14, 1882-April 27, 1904) is the most dramatic funerary art in Crown Hill. The Forrest sculpture grieves inside a three-sided Greek structure made of granite with benches along the side walls. (Section 25, Lot 230)

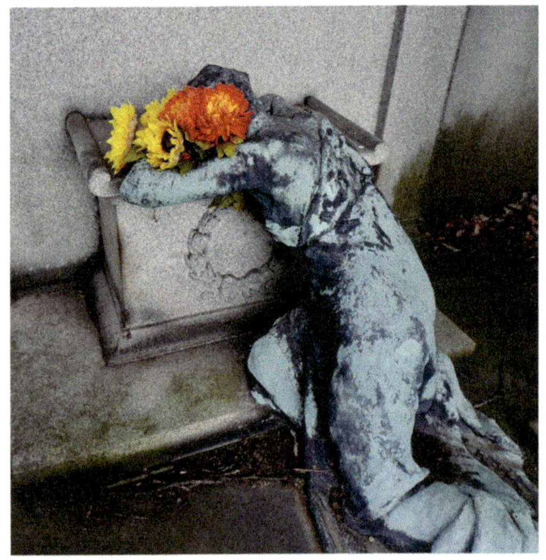

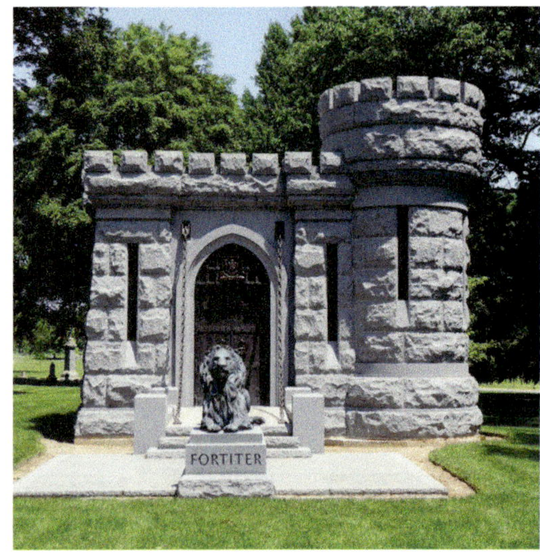

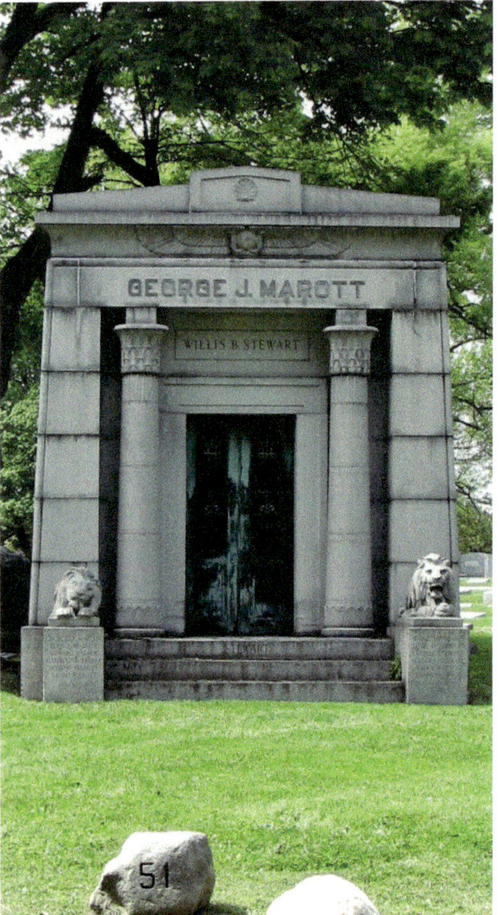

Above left: At the monument for Albertina Allen Forrest, the bronze female figure weeps as she kneels on a granite step holding a palm leaf that symbolizes victory over death. The epitaph reads, "A loss forever new, a void where heart on heart reposed, and where warm hands have prest and closed. Silence." (Section 25, Lot 230)

Above right: The Fortiter Castle Mausoleum is a future resting place for the Fortiter family. Built in 2023 of granite, and custom-designed by Gibraltar Mausoleum Services of Indianapolis, construction took about a year. The mausoleum can accommodate up to twelve interments (Section 67, Lot 365)

Left: George Joseph Marott (Dec 10, 1858 - Feb 15, 1946) has a popular mausoleum that was built in the Egyptian style. Two stone lions take turns guarding the crypt: one lion sleeps while the other keeps watch.

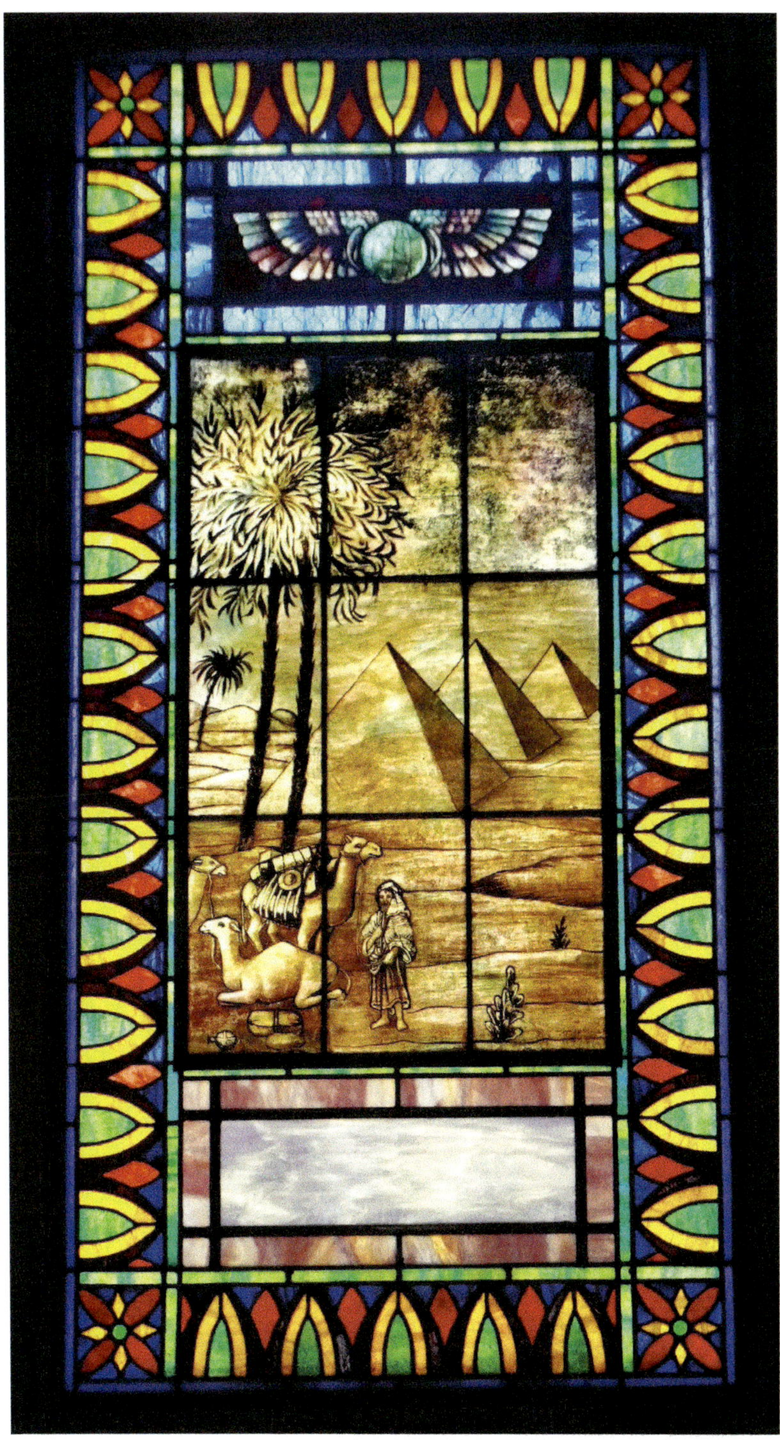

Inside the Marrott mausoleum, the stained-glass window depicts an Egyptian scene with pyramids, camels, and palm trees. (Section 51, Lot 247)

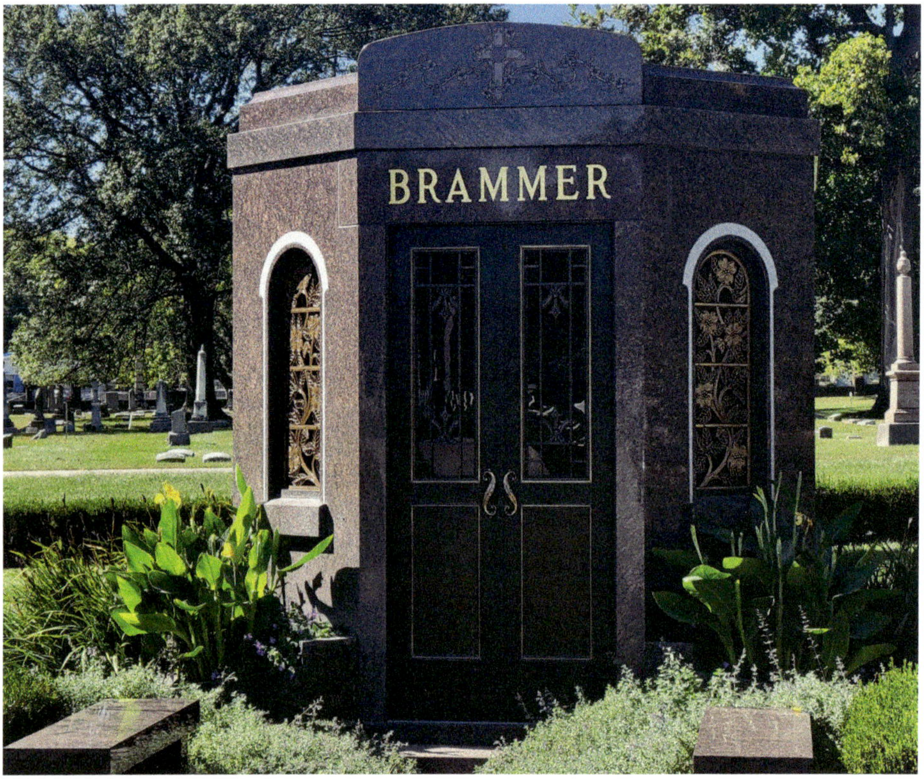

The Brammer Mausoleum is the future resting place for members of the Brammer family. It was built in 2023 by Gibraltar Mausoleum Services, owned by Jay Brammer. It is constructed of granite in an octagonal shape, with detailed floral artwork at the windows. (Section 9, Lot 1)

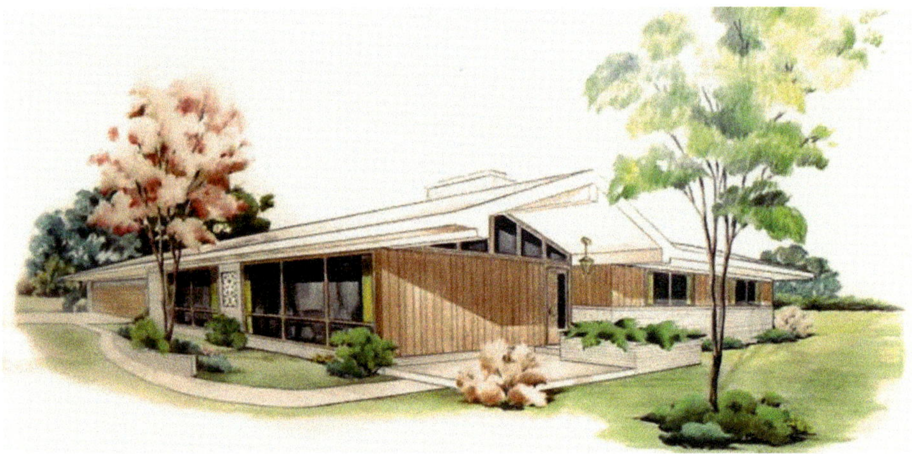

Avriel Joy Christie Shull (February 9, 1931 – March 6, 1976) was a groundbreaking architectural designer known for her mid-century modern designs built in Marion and Hamilton Counties. Her cremains rest in a book-shaped box in her glass-fronted crypt. (Community Mausoleum, Niche D-47) [Cubed]

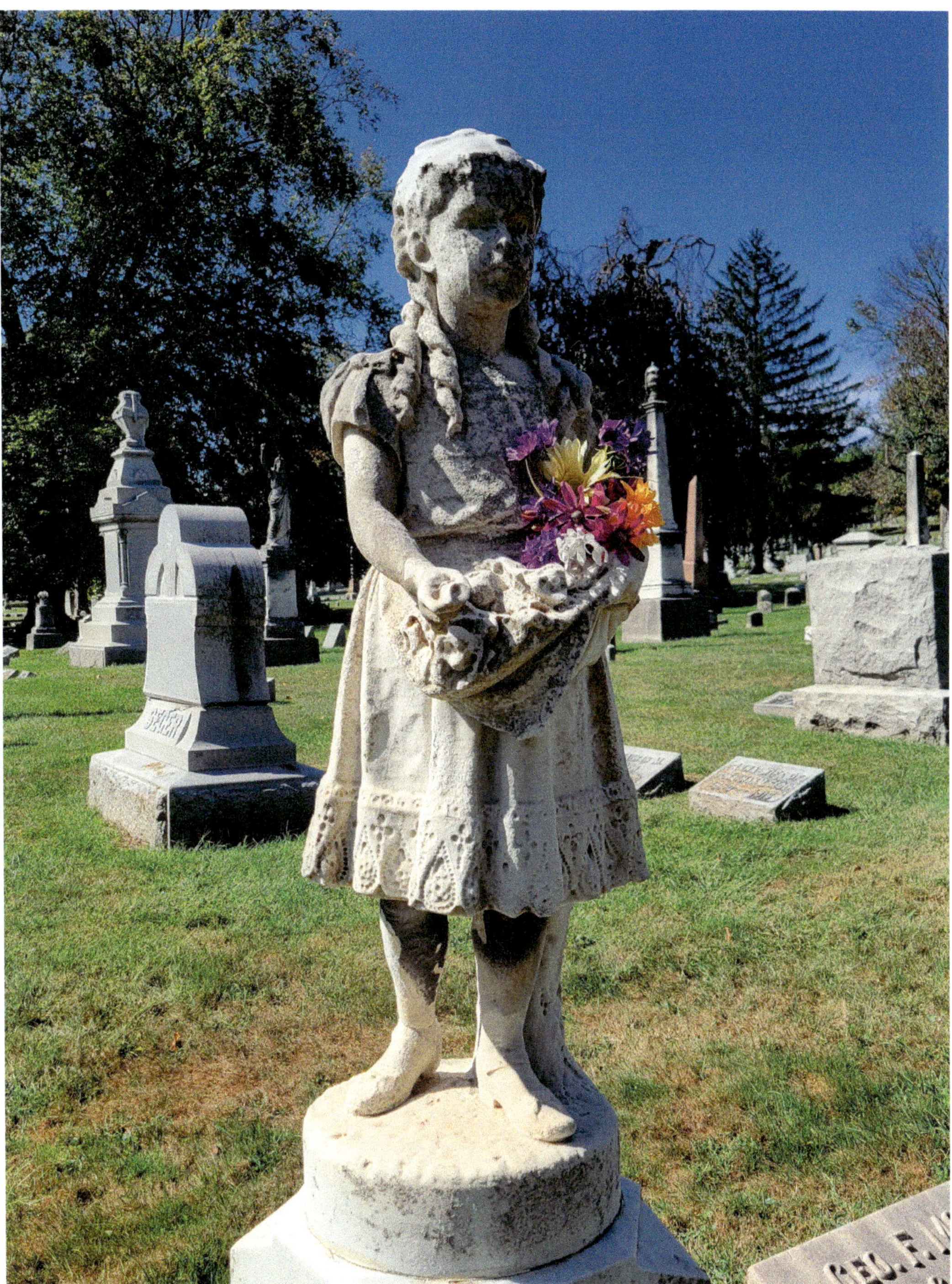

Mary Ella McGinnis (December 15, 1869 – August 6, 1875) was five-years-old when she died from lung congestion. Visitors leave real flowers in Mary Ella's arms in remembrance of her short life. (Section 16, Lot 23) *[Alessa Kivlehen]*

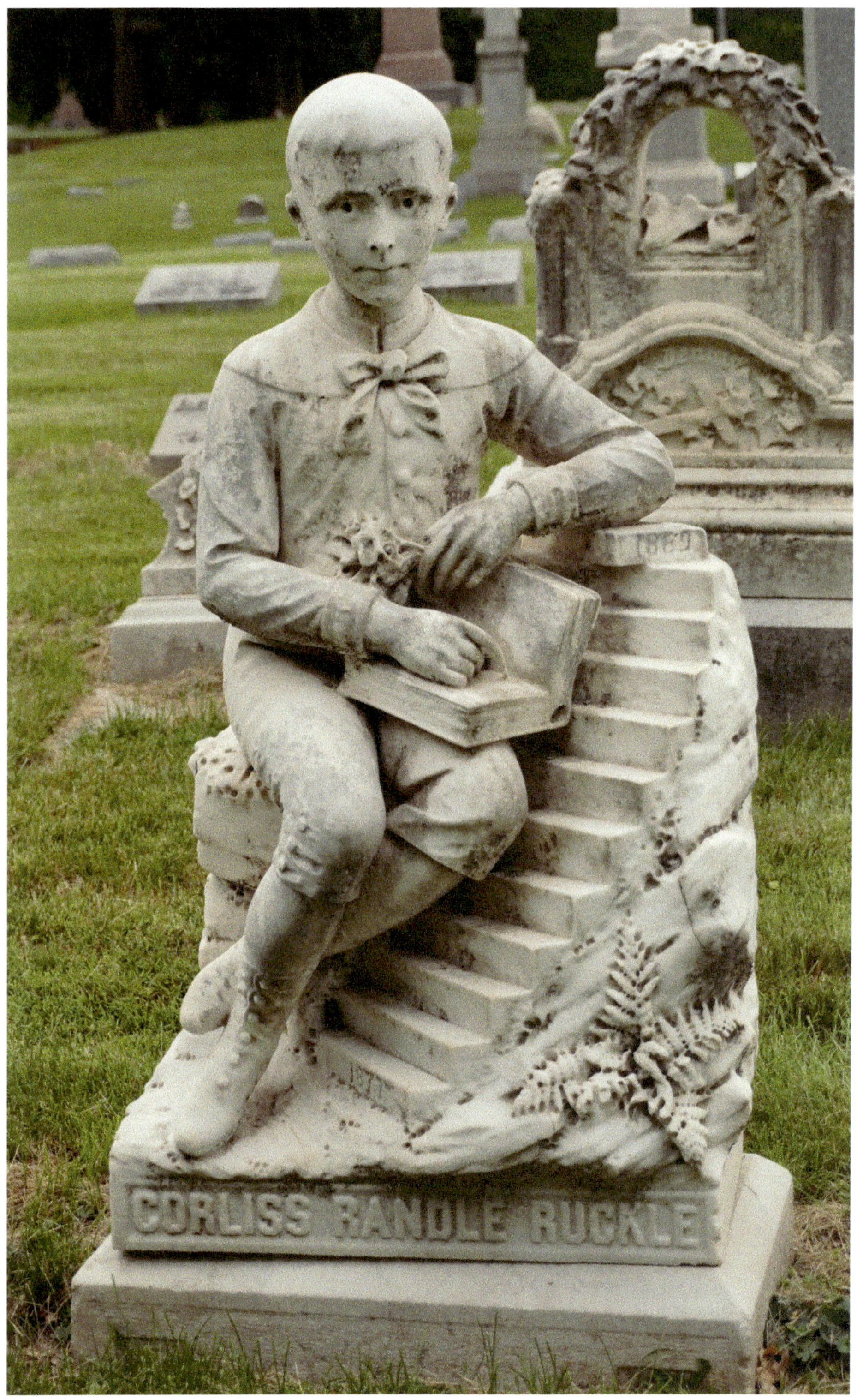
CORLISS RANDLE RUCKLE

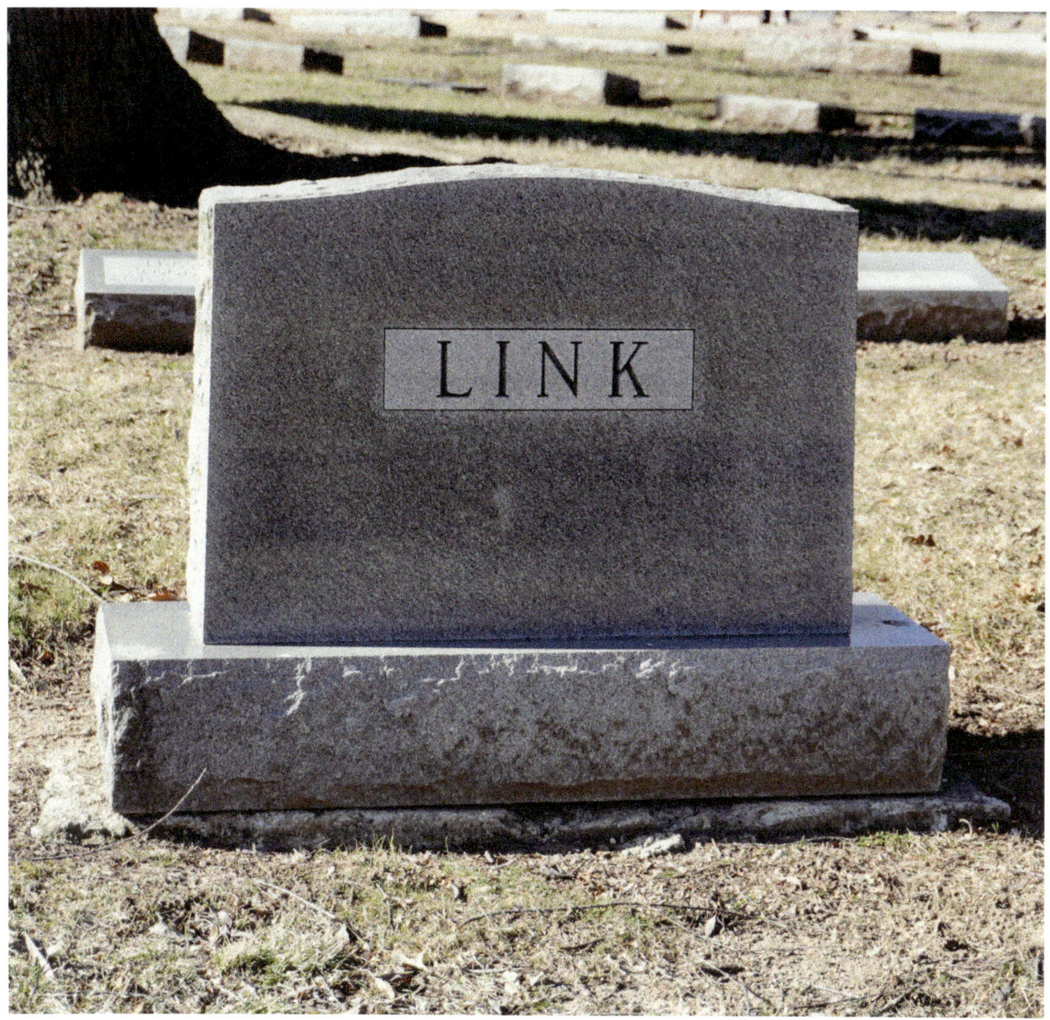

Helen Essie Kegerreis Link (August 24, 1912 – November 30, 2002) became a well-known authority on daffodils, promoting and cultivating them throughout the country. Family headstones surround the large grey granite marker. (Section 67, Lot 82)

Opposite page: Corliss Randle Ruckle (December 19, 1877 – December 4, 1889) died at the age of eleven from the "strangling angel," diphtheria. His life-sized statue, dressed in late-nineteenth-century style, rests his arm on the eleventh step of a marble staircase. Corliss holds his "Book of Life," pointing to indicate his short mortality. (Section 12, Lot 24)

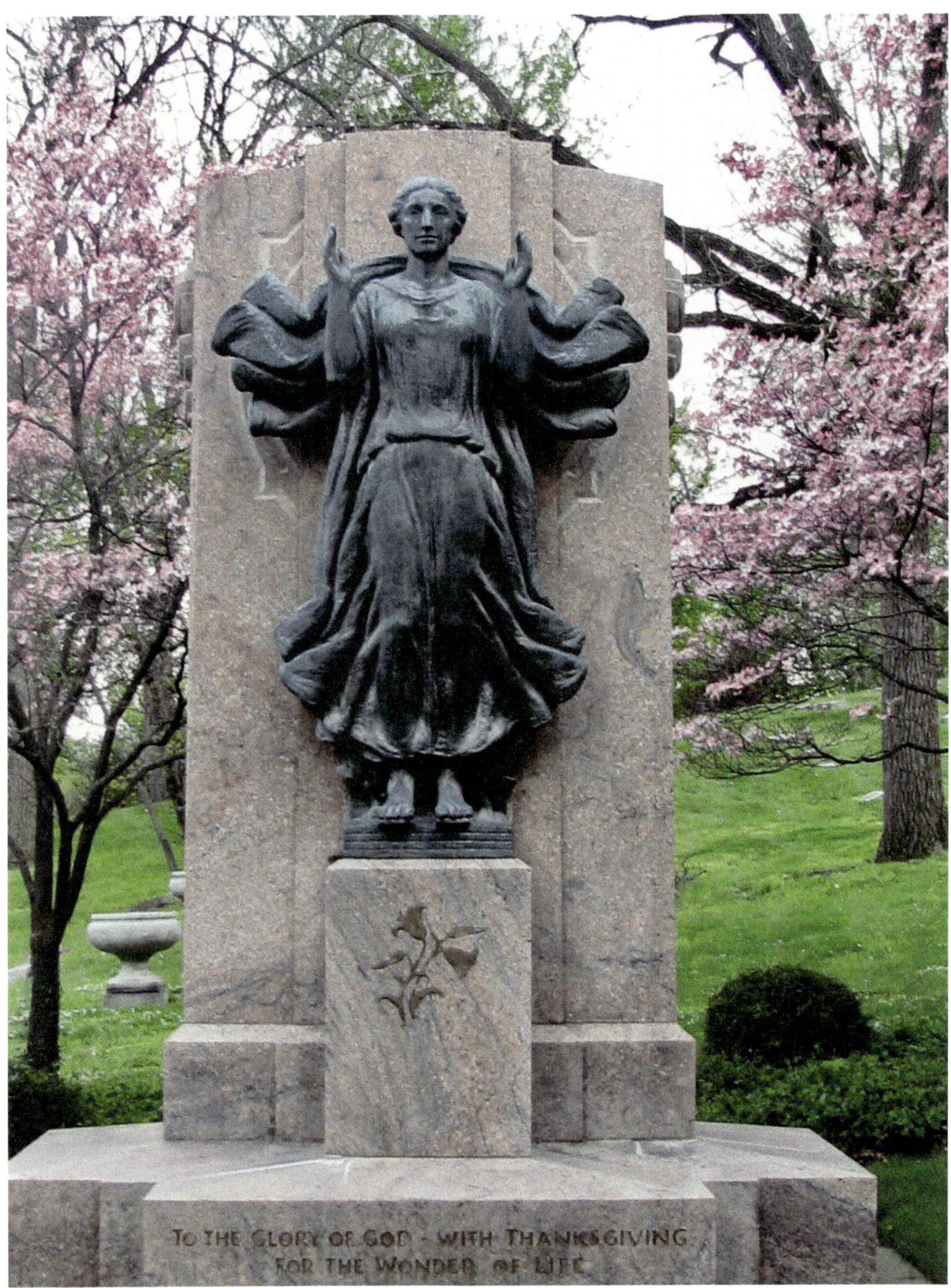

There are twin angels located in Crown Hill. A bronze statue stands backed with pink granite at the Eli Lilly monument. The epitaph reads, “To the glory of God – with thanksgiving for the wonder of life.” (Section 13)

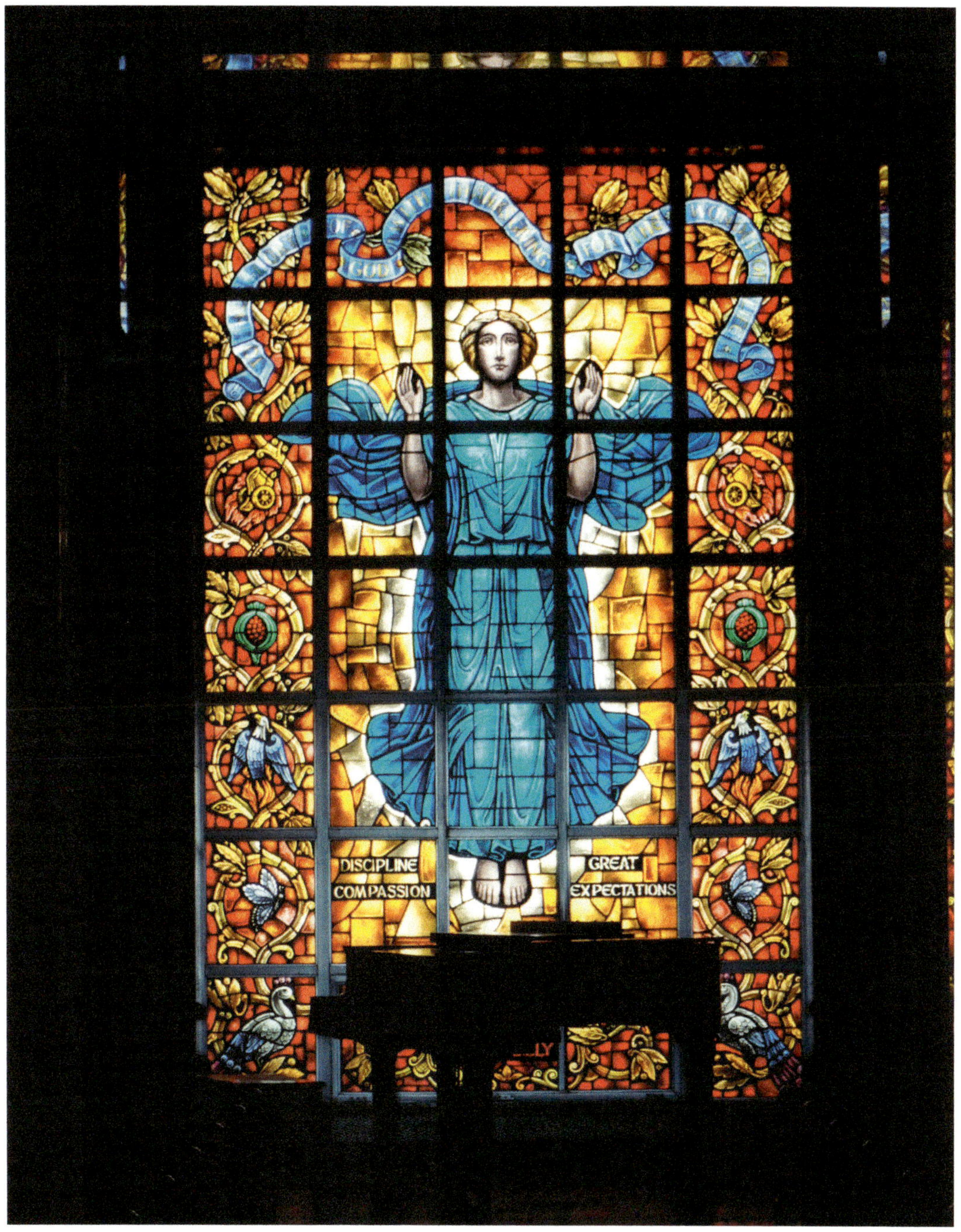

The matching stained-glass angel is vibrantly colored with the words, "Discipline, Compassion, and Great Expectations" at her feet. A grand piano sits in front of the window in the Peace Chapel of the Community Mausoleum. Both angels designate burial places for members of the Lilly family. (North Grounds)

14

The Famous Buildings of Crown Hill

The historic designs of Crown Hill's architecture add beauty and grace to the cemetery. Gothic Revival style dominates the main structures, with pointed arches, ornate patterns, and stained-glass windows. Romanesque Revival features round arches, heavy stonework, and simplified ornamentation for a sturdier appearance. Both styles give the cemetery a High Victorian appearance.

The Gothic Chapel, built in 1875, was originally called the Gothic Vault. Built of Hoosier limestone in the Gothic Revival style, it was designed by architect Diedrich August Bohlen, the first trained architect in Indianapolis. Bohlen built the Gothic Chapel in a cruciform shape. The central chapel stands two stories tall and can temporarily hold ninety-six remains. The Gothic Chapel is listed on the National Register of Historic Places.

In 1885, the Gothic Gate and Waiting Station were constructed of Indiana limestone and feature three arched entryways. The Waiting Station, trimmed with limestone, was where people met and waited for funerals. Architect Adolph Scherrer was skilled at blending different architectural styles to create more innovative designs. Scherrer served on the first Indianapolis Board of Public Works in 1891 to help maintain and oversee the city's development. The Gothic Gate was finished in time for the funeral procession of Vice President Thomas A. Hendricks.

Designed in the Romanesque Revival style, the Main West Gate consisted of a large archway connecting two buildings. The two-story structure and chapel-like building were all constructed of Indiana limestone. The gateway was built in 1901 but was closed and demolished in 1965 to make way for Interstate 65. Indianapolis architect Herbert Foltz designed the Main West Gate. He served on the board of the Indianapolis Public Schools and was president of the League of American Wheelmen.

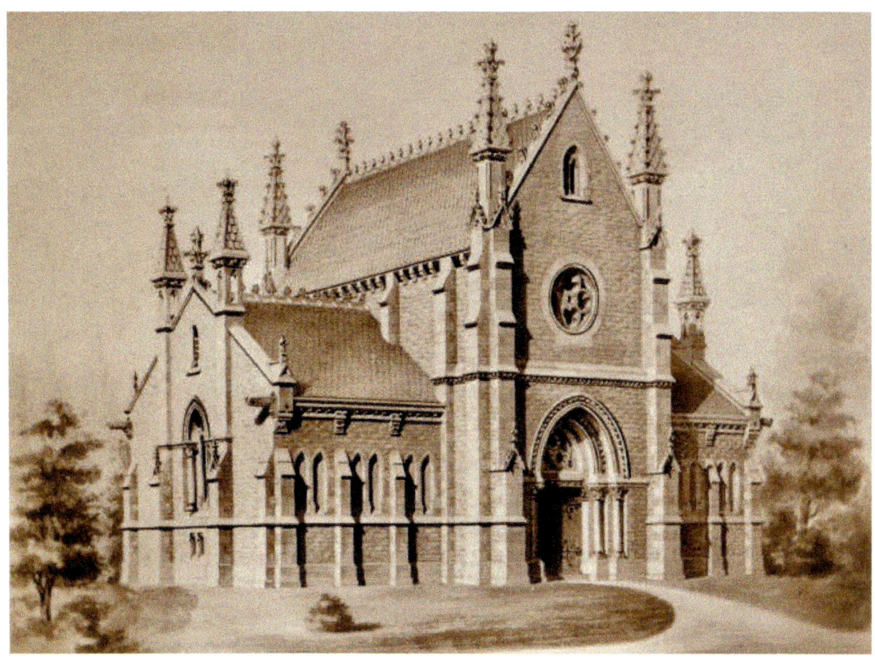

Originally called the Gothic Vault, the Gothic Chapel was designed in the Gothic Revival style in 1875. This photo is from 1917. (Section 9) *[Indiana Historical Society]*

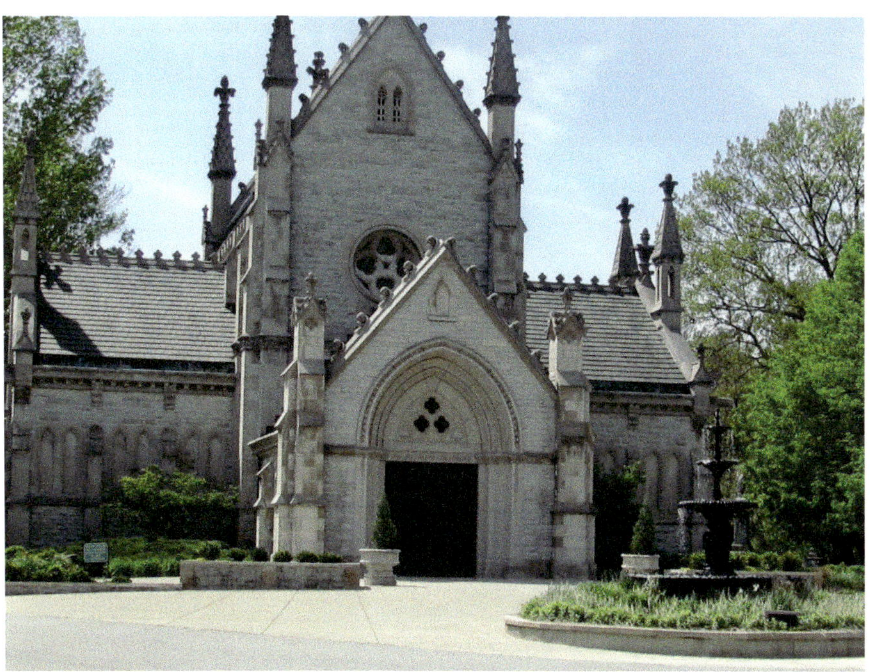

Today, the majestic Gothic Chapel hosts weddings, funerals, events, concerts, and dinners. It is listed on the National Register of Historic Places.

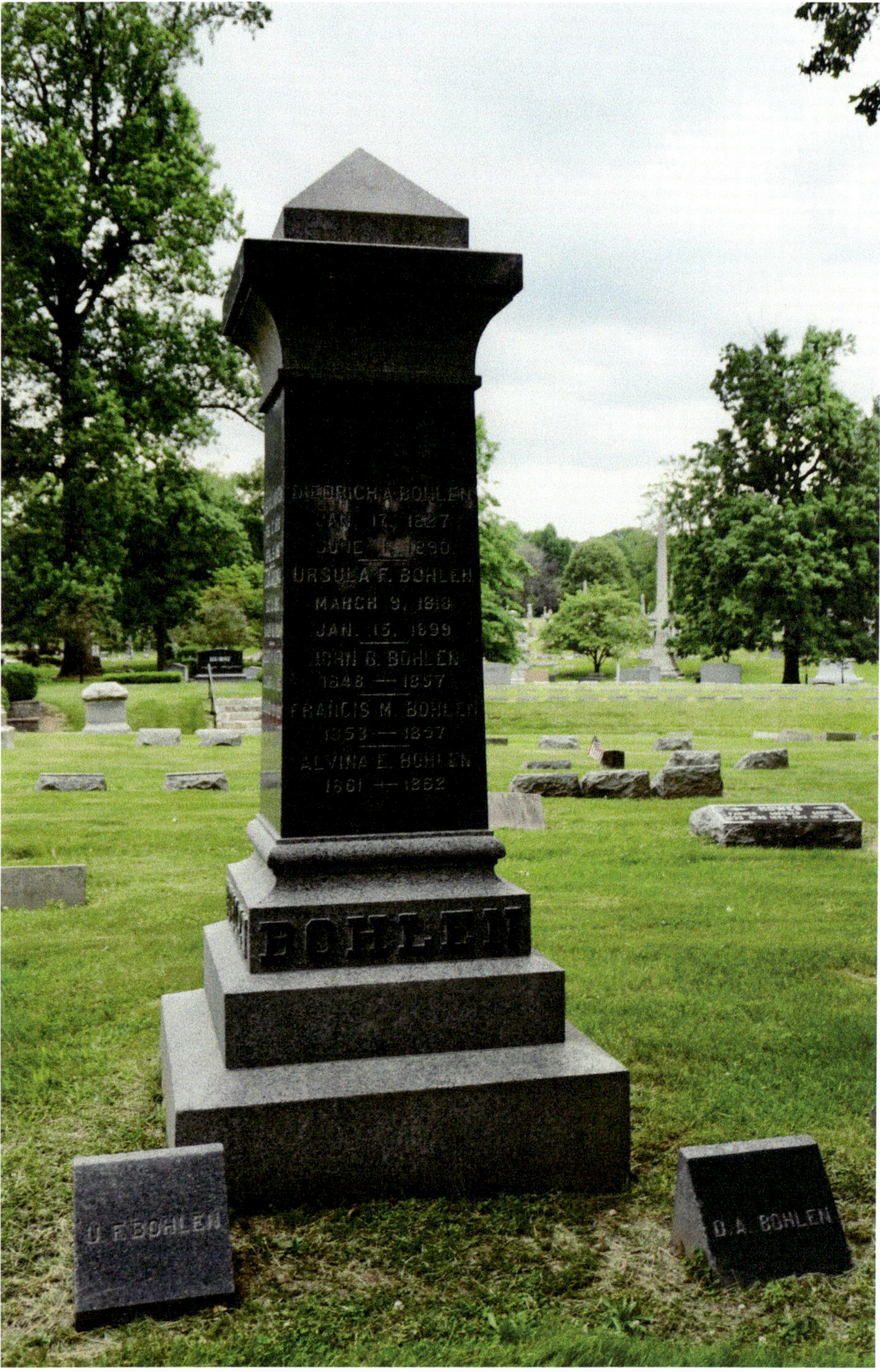

Architect Diedrich August Bohlen (January 17, 1827 – June 1, 1890) designed the Gothic Chapel in 1875. (Section 25, Lot 177)

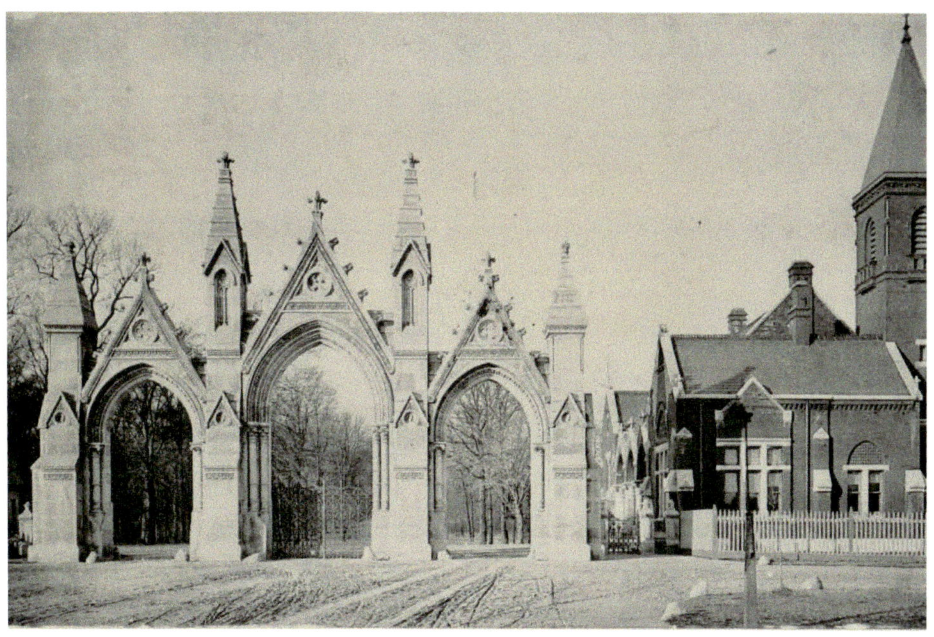

The Gothic Gate and Waiting Station was designed in the Gothic Revival style by Adolph Scherrer in 1885. (Originally at 34th and Boulevard Place, now the south entrance) *[Indiana Historical Society]*

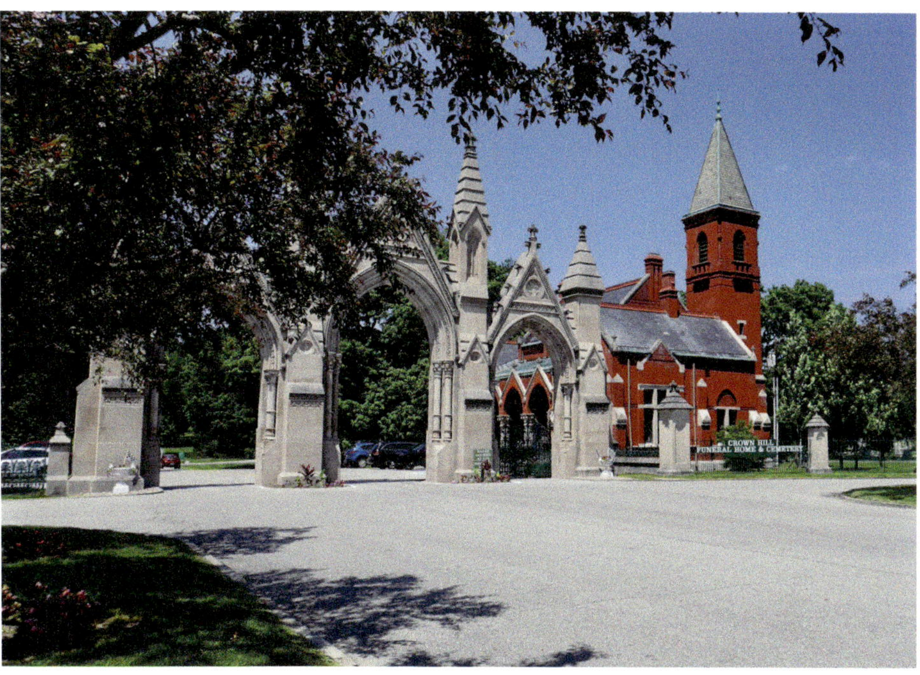

The Gothic Gate and Waiting Station remain a stunning entrance into Crown Hill and continues to hold a place of prominence in the cemetery.

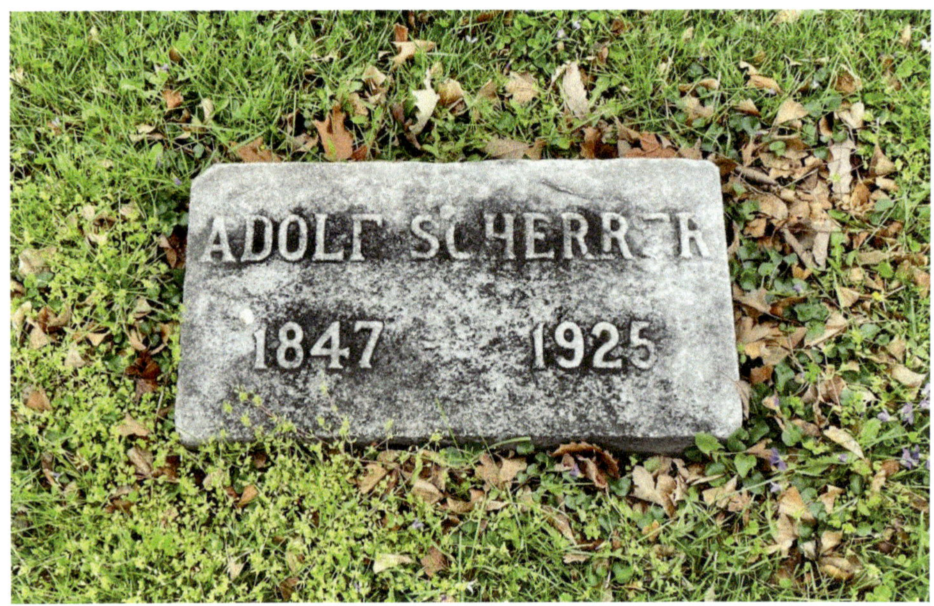

Architect Adolph Scherrer (August 30, 1847 – February 13, 1925) designed the cemetery's Gothic Gate and Waiting Station. (Section 53, Lot 201)

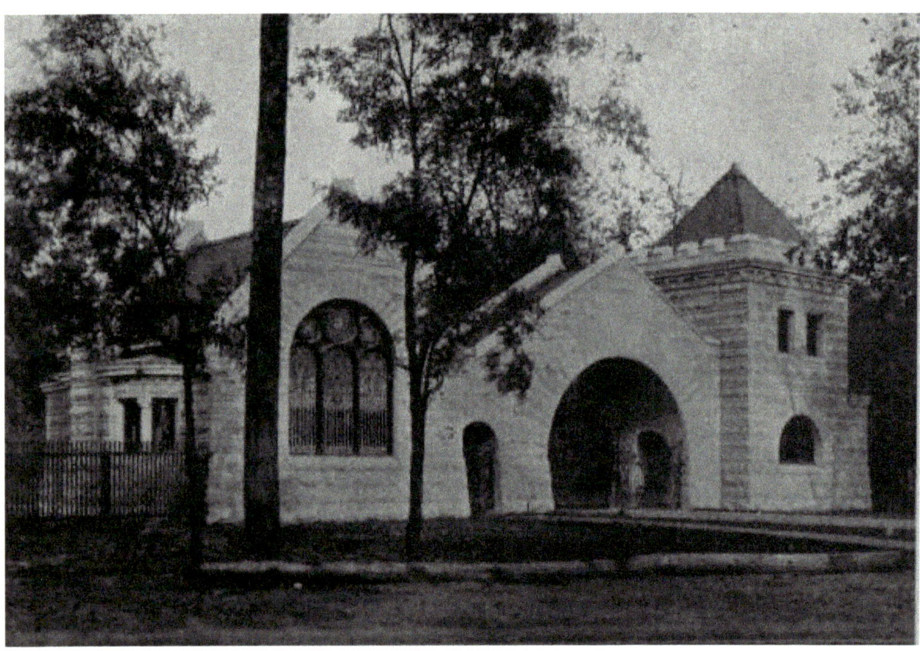

The Main West Entrance to Crown Hill Cemetery was designed in the Romanesque Revival style by architect Herbert Foltz (February 23, 1867 – July 6, 1946), pictured in the drive in 1901. This entrance was torn down in 1965 to make way for an interstate. (Foltz: Section 13, Lot 8) *[Indiana Album: Evan Finch Collection]*

15

Those Buried "On the Crown"

The summit of Crown Hill offers a gorgeous view of the city's skyline and surrounding region. This place of prominence provides a connection to the historical and cultural aspects of the community. It is considered an honor and distinction to be buried in this picturesque and serene location.

Indianapolis resident Larry Allyn Conrad served as Indiana secretary of state from 1970 to 1978. He played a key role in drafting the Twenty-fifth Amendment detailing the line of succession if the president is incapacitated.

Entrepreneur William Francis Bane founded a residential and commercial carpet cleaning company, which developed the first truck-mounted carpet cleaning machine in 1970.

Businessman Russell Fortune, Sr., started a wood veneer business that imported and produced high-quality wood veneers. The company became a respected name in the wood veneer industry.

Businessman Robert "Bob" Irsay brought the NFL's Colts from Baltimore to Indianapolis. Irsay utilized a hands-on approach with the team and the community to the benefit of both.

Engineer Louise Schwitzer won the first auto race held at the Indianapolis Motor Speedway in 1909 and later served on the Indianapolis Motor Speedway Technical Committee. The "Louis Schwitzer Award for Design Innovation" is presented annually after each Indianapolis 500 race.

Thomas W. Binford was involved in industry, civil rights, and racing. He was instrumental in helping to bring the Colts football team to Indianapolis and served as the Chief Steward of the Indianapolis 500 from 1974 to 1995.

Stanley Malless became co-owner of Indy racecars for drivers Jim Hurtubise and Eddie Sachs during the 1960s. Malless was well-known throughout the world of tennis as a tournament champion and president of the Central Indiana Tennis Association, Western Tennis Association, and United States Tennis Association.

Philanthropist Harrison Eiteljorg began exhibiting his Western and Native Art collections at the Indianapolis Museum of Art. In 1989, he founded the Eiteljorg

Museum of American Indians and Western Art in Indianapolis, the only midwestern museum to showcase Native American and Western artifacts and artwork.

Poet James Whitcomb Riley was a best-selling author known as the "Hoosier Poet" and the "Children's Poet." His works include *Little Orphan Annie* and *The Raggedy Man*, which celebrated growing up in rural Indiana.

Composer EmCele Torgersen Masbaum published her organ compositions through the American Society of Composers, Authors, and Publishers (ASCAP) and the American Guild of Organists (AGO).

Herbert E. Strong, Jr. marked his grave with a granite picnic table that encourages passersby to sit and reflect, fulfilling his lifelong desire to bring people together.

A bronze statue of a boy sitting on a bench engraved with "Home Sweet Home" marks the graves of Herbert Sweet and Delores (Dee) McDaniel Sweet. In 1933, they started Little Acorn Day Camp near Carmel, Indiana. It was the first "day-camp" in the United States. The Sweet's son-in-law, Mic Mead, carved the sculpture.

Crown Hill Cemetery is a marvelous place to explore where history, art, and nature come together in a tranquil setting to provide a sense of community and impart cultural significance for current and future generations to enjoy.

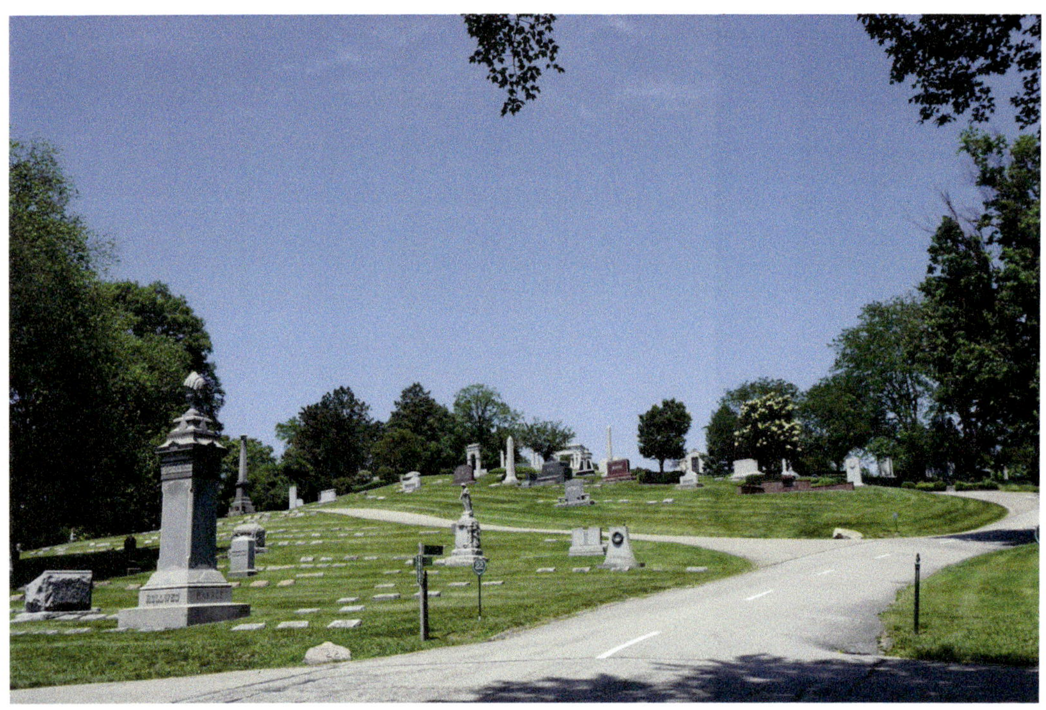

"On the Crown" is a special place in the cemetery, and burial here is an honor. Many of Indianapolis's prominent citizens are interred in this serene and captivating location.

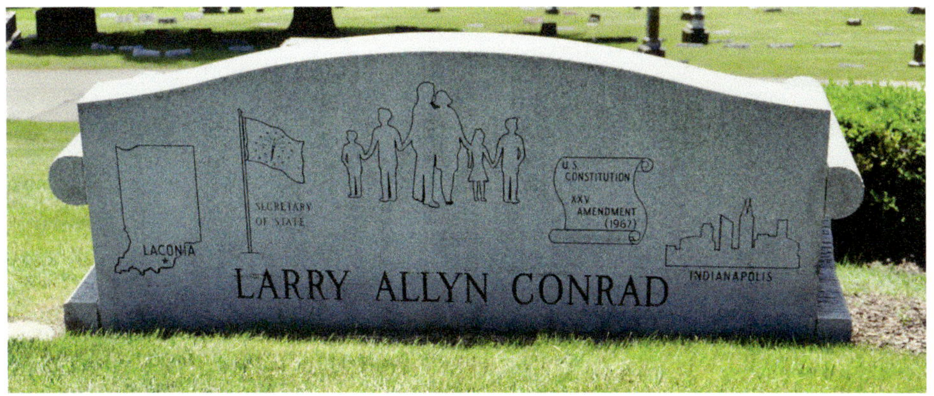

Secretary of State Larry A. Conrad (February 8, 1935-July 7, 1990) was a notable politician and civic leader. His grave is marked by a family bench with the Conrad family history etched on the back. (Section 88, Lot 14, On the Crown)

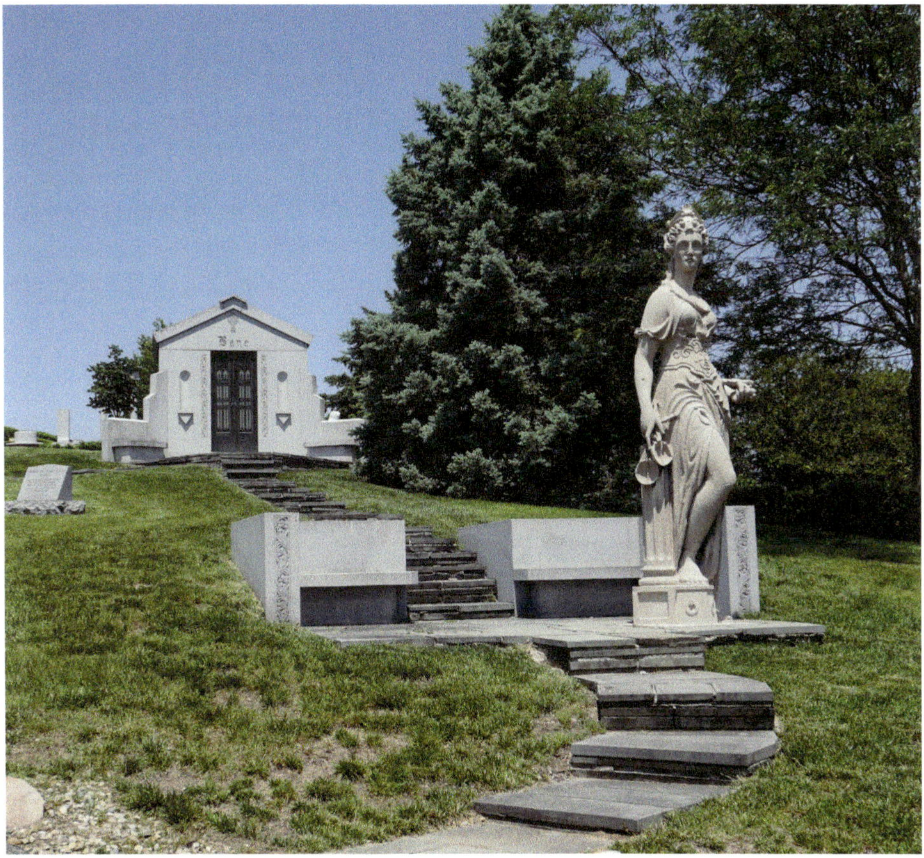

William Francis Bane (June 25, 1927 – February 20, 2014) founded the William F. Bane Company in 1962. The Greek goddess Themis stands at the entrance to the Bane Mausoleum. Themis represents divine law and justice in Greek mythology. (Section 46, Lot 1, On the Crown)

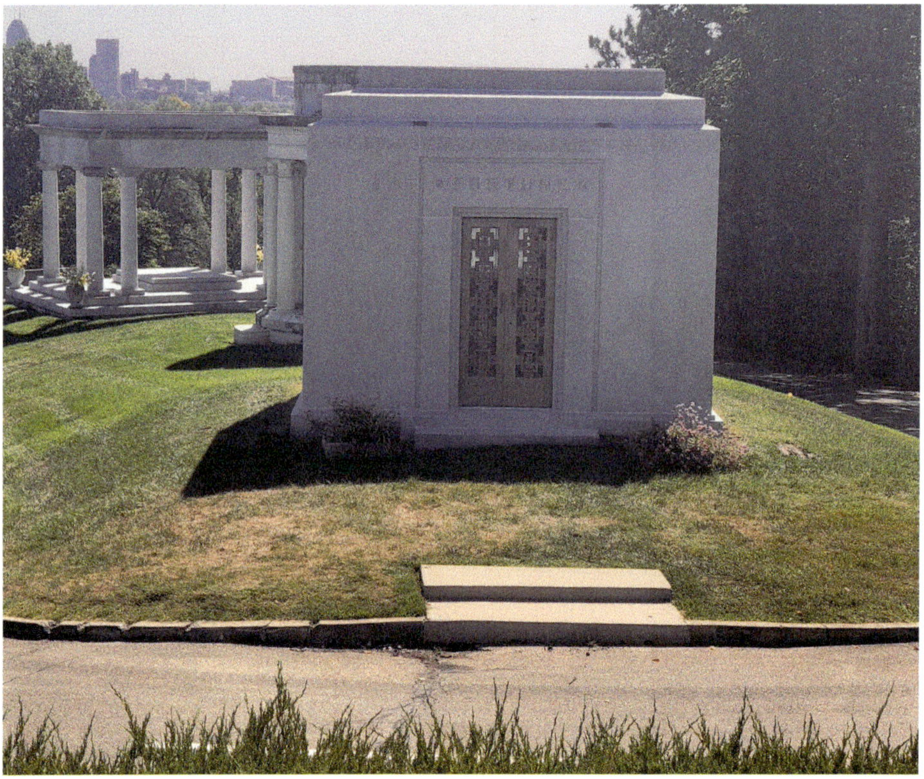

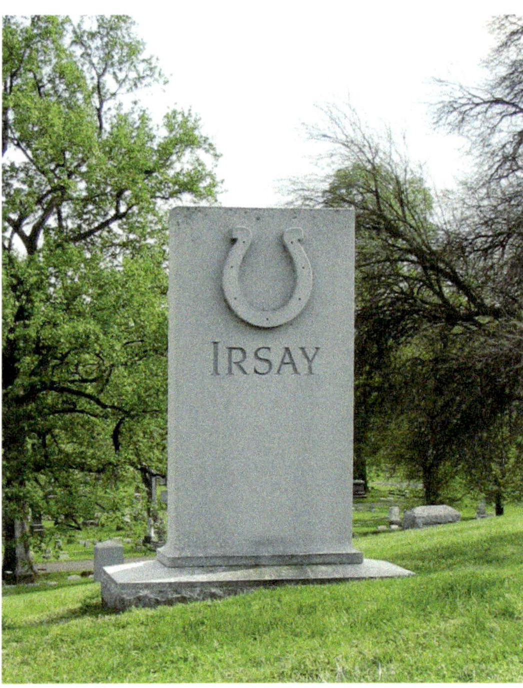

Above: Russell Fortune, Sr. (September 12, 1885 – August 2, 1970) was an Indianapolis businessman who became a well-known producer of wood veneers. The Fortune mausoleum is built in the modern style, with double bronze doors that face away from the city skyline. (Section 61, Lot 2, On the Crown) *[Alessa Kivlehen]*

Left: Robert "Bob" Irsay (March 5, 1923 – January 14, 1997) purchased the Baltimore Colts and moved the team to Indianapolis. His monument features a horseshoe to signify his allegiance with the Indianapolis Colts football team. (Section 88, Lot 5, On the Crown)

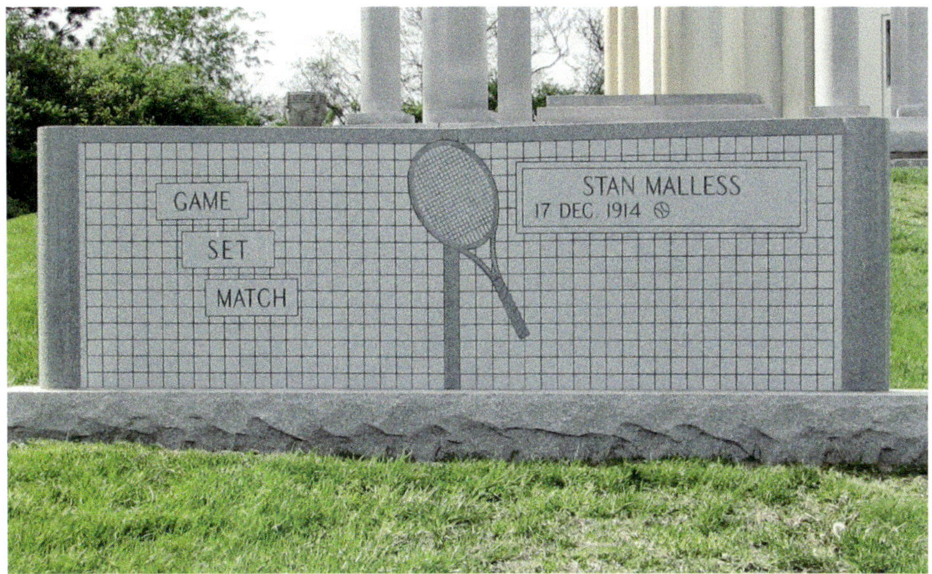

Stanley Malless (December 17, 1914 – January 19, 2012) was a tennis tournament champion. His monument depicts a granite tennis net engraved with the game's scoring terms: Game, Set, Match. (Section 61, Lot 5, On the Crown)

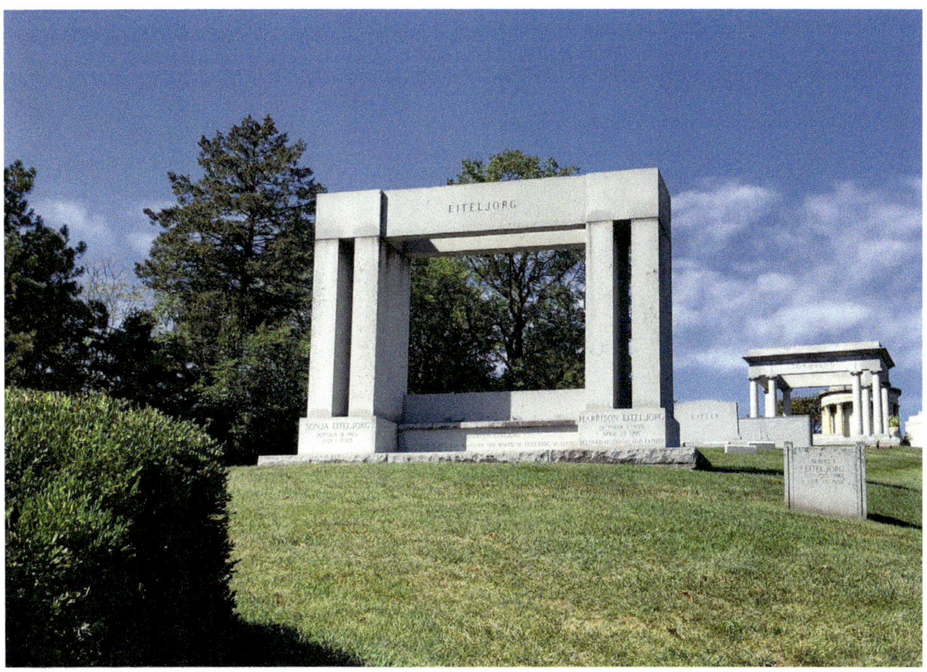

Harrison Eiteljorg (October 1, 1903 – April 29, 199) was a Native American and Western art collector who founded the Eiteljorg Museum. His modern monument is open with a bench provided between the double pillars. (Section 61, Lot 8, On the Crown)

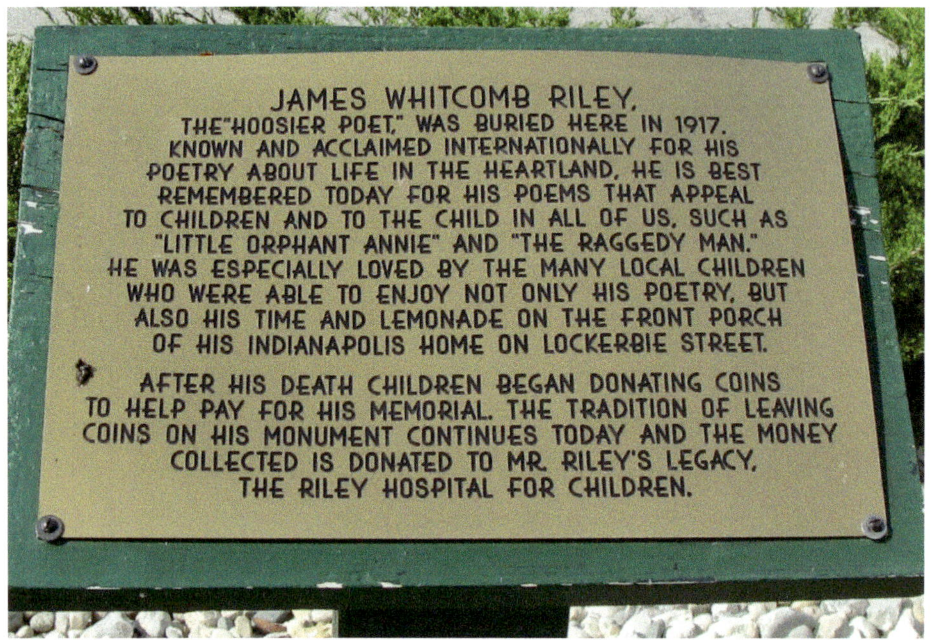

James Whitcomb Riley (October 7, 1849 – July 22, 1916) was known as the "The Hoosier Poet." Children's pennies helped to build his memorial. Today, coins collected from his gravesite go to Riley Children's Hospital, which was named after him. (Section 61, Lot 1, On the Crown)

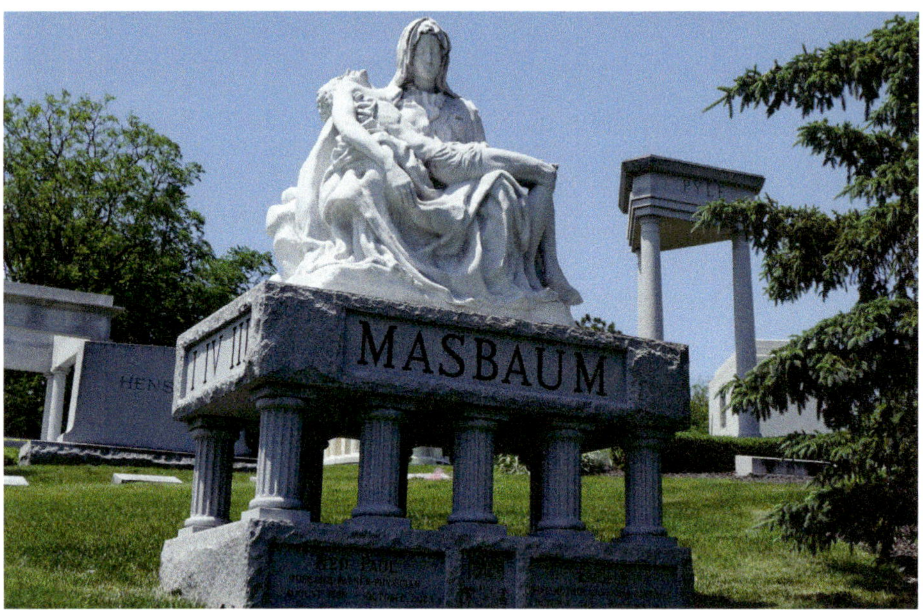

Composer EmCele Torgersen Masbaum (October 1940 – December 2014) was a published Indiana composer. Her monument is topped with a sculpture of Mary holding the wounded Jesus. A treble clef is carved beside her name. (Section 61, Lot 21, On the Crown)

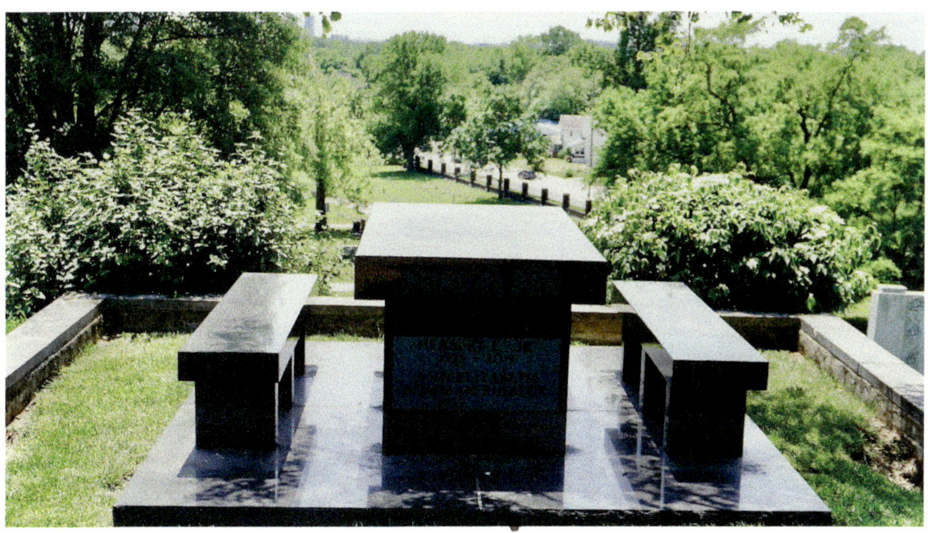

Herbert E. Strong, Jr. (October 2, 1925 – June 24, 2015) was a respected businessman in Indianapolis. The granite picnic table provides a pleasant place to sit in the cemetery while enjoying a view of the city skyline. (Section 88, Lot 15, On the Crown)

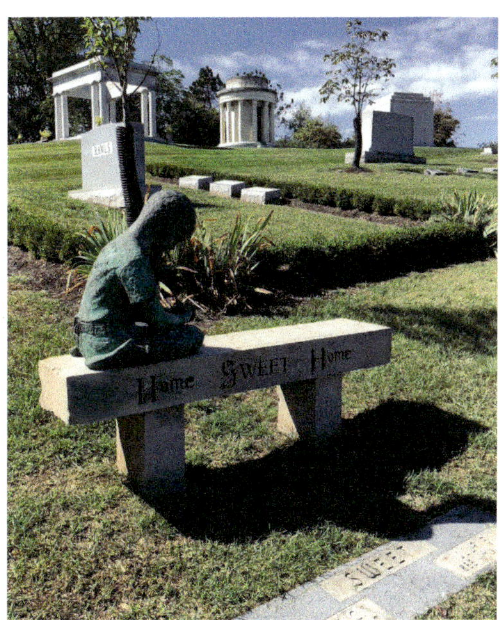

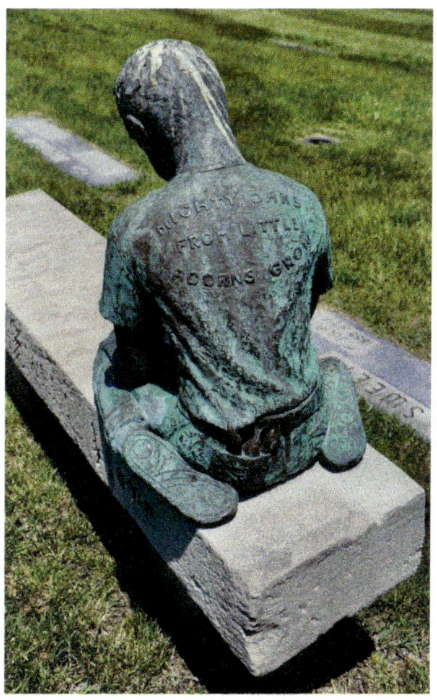

Above left: Herbert (November 17, 1908 – July 20, 200) and Delores (Dee) (June 3, 1913 – October 21, 200) Sweet's graves are marked with a small bench bearing the words, "Home Sweet Home" in honor of the first day-camp, Little Acorn, that they started near Carmel, Indiana in 1933.

Above right: The bronze statue of a young boy sits on the Sweet bench contemplating an acorn he holds. The back of his shirt reads, "Might oaks from little acorns grow." (Section 61, Lot 18, On the Crown)

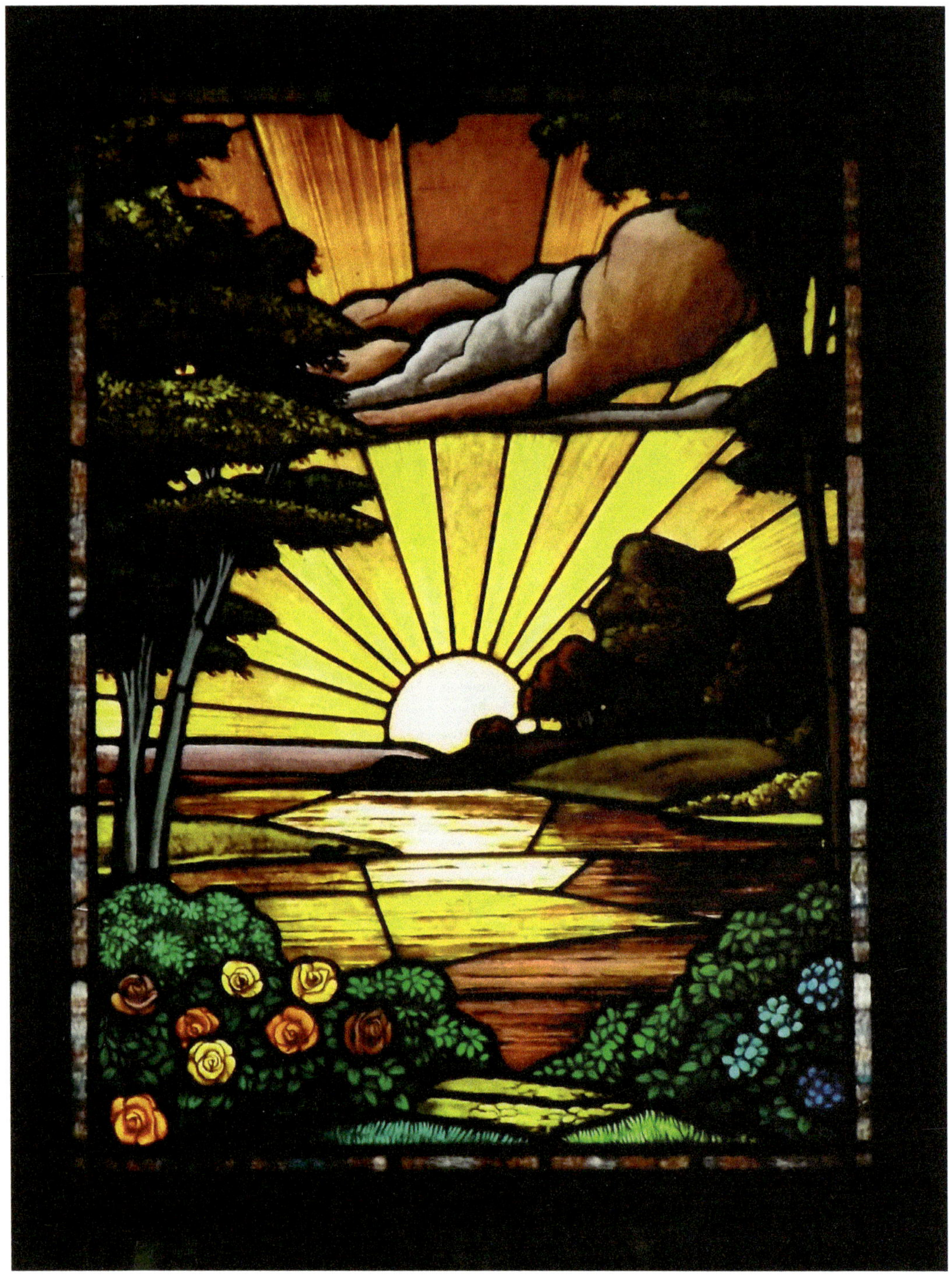

"Sunset on Stained Glass" is a brilliant window in the Peace Chapel of the Crown Hill Community Mausoleum, and a fitting end to our time spent at *Crown Hill Cemetery: The City on a Hill*. (North Grounds)